THE JESUS
OF
HERESY AND HISTORY

The Discovery and Meaning
of the Nag Hammadi Gnostic Library

JOHN DART

1817

Harper & Row, Publishers, San Francisco

Cambridge, Hagerstown, New York, Philadelphia, Washington
London, Mexico City, São Paulo, Singapore, Sydney

This is a revised and expanded edition of *The Laughing Savior: The Discovery and Significance of the Nag Hammadi Gnostic Library*.

THE JESUS OF HERESY AND HISTORY: The Discovery and Meaning of the Nag Hammadi Gnostic Library. Copyright © 1988 by John Dart. All rights reserved. Printed in the United States of America. No part of this book may be used or reproduced in any manner whatsoever without written permission except in the case of brief quotations embodied in critical articles and reviews. For information address Harper & Row, Publishers, Inc., 10 East 53rd Street, New York, NY 10022. Published simultaneously in Canada by Fitzhenry & Whiteside, Limited, Toronto.

FIRST EDITION

Library of Congress Cataloging-in-Publication Data
Dart, John, 1936-
  The Jesus of heresy and history.

  Rev. and expanded ed of: The Laughing Savior. 1976.
  Bibliography: p.
  Includes index.
  1. Nag Hammadi codices. 2. Gnosticism. 3. Jesus
Christ—Gnostic interpretations. I. Dart, John,
1936–   . Laughing Savior. II. Title.
BT1391.D36 1988   299′.932   88–45131
ISBN 0–06–061691–1 (hard)
ISBN 0–06–061694–6 (pbk.)

88 89 90 91 92 HC 10 9 8 7 6 5 4 3 2 1

To Gloria with love

Contents

Illustrations

Preface

This book updates and expands *The Laughing Savior: The Discovery and Significance of the Nag Hammadi Gnostic Library*, published in 1976, also by Harper & Row. The most thorough revision has been made in Parts III and IV, but no chapter has been left unchanged.

The earlier version was undertaken when few people other than specialists in the field were acquainted with the fascinating story of the manuscripts. In addition, the new "gospels" and several other intriguing works in the library had been published and discussed but rarely accompanied by a popularly written overview.

One handicap to understanding was the fact not all of the texts had been published by that time. With the kind assistance of the translators and editors connected with the Institute for Antiquity and Christianity, Claremont, California, I attempted to provide an introduction to the discovery and contents. An important milestone was reached in late 1977, sooner than expected, when Harper & Row (with E. J. Brill, Co.) published *The Nag Hammadi Library in English*, with a short introduction for each book.

Since then, new perspectives on the Gnostic movement and Christian origins have emerged, some early scholarly insights have been strengthened with further study, and some interpretations have lost favor. Most remarkably, Nag Hammadi's *Gospel of Thomas* has been established as an indispensable tool for assessment of the historical Jesus.

When Harper & Row decided to publish an updated edition of *The Nag Hammadi Library in English*, again under the general editorship of James M. Robinson, publisher Clayton Carlson graciously asked me if I would revise and expand my 1976 book so that it could be released at the same time. We revised the title too. The image of "the laughing savior" is, after all, but one element in Gnostic myth making, although an important one. In the final analysis, the Nag Hammadi library is most famous for

The Gospel of Thomas and other texts contributing to a historical understanding of how Christianity's founder was variously viewed from earliest times.

I wrote both editions as a news reporter. The Nag Hammadi discovery and contents struck me as a good story not long after I started on the religion news beat for the *Los Angeles Times* in 1967. I was able to do the research for the first edition during a professional journalistic fellowship at Stanford University in 1973–1974, funded primarily by the National Endowment for the Humanities. My Stanford studies were aided greatly by the late William A. Clebsch and Robert Hamerton-Kelly. Scholars who helped me make sense out of the Gnostic texts included James M. Robinson, James Brashler, Birger Pearson, the late George MacRae, Charles Hedrick, Pheme Perkins, and Helmut Koester. While he was working in Ethiopia during government turmoil in 1974–1975, Jean Doresse supplied me with colorful details on the discovery by correspondence.

After *The Laughing Savior* was published, I continued my interest in *The Gospel of Thomas* and New Testament studies. I was accepted as a member of the Society of Biblical Literature in 1979 and have read a half dozen papers at annual sessions of the society's Pacific Coast region.

My research was conducted independently of my job at the *Los Angeles Times*, but with that acquired knowledge newsworthy developments in biblical studies became more discernible.

Innumerable scholars have allowed me to try their patience with my questions and ideas. My thanks to them. Thanks also go to Tom Grady, my editor for this expanded version. And special gratitude to my wife, Gloria, and my children, Kim, John, Randall, and Christopher.

Introduction

Shortly after World War II the secret scriptures of two historically obscure religious movements were discovered in the Middle
East. One discovery was the Dead Sea Scrolls of the Essenes, a
Jewish sect that endured until 68 c.e. (Common Era). The other
find was the Nag Hammadi Gnostic library, a collection of fifty-
two religious texts written on papyrus sheets cut and bound into
book form. Though the library was found near the Upper Nile
city of Nag Hammadi (pronounced Nahg Ha-MAH-Dee) in
Egypt, the Gnostic beliefs found in the books once were widespread in the Mediterranean lands.

Gnostics were both internal and external rivals of early Christianity, especially in the second century. Sometimes called Gnostics by unfriendly critics in the churches, they claimed to have
an esoteric *gnosis* (Greek, "knowledge") far superior to that of
other religious and philosophic groups. (The same root is apparent in the word *agnostic*, one who disclaims any knowledge
or any capability of knowledge of God.) From both the Dead Sea
Scrolls and the Nag Hammadi Gnostic library, scholars expected
not only to hear those long-dead religious movements finally tell
their own stories but also to obtain unparalleled new insights into
the formative years of today's rabbinic Judaism and its giant offspring, Christianity.

The content and significance of the Dead Sea Scrolls was
generally known and appreciated by the late 1950s, but the
world has had to wait longer for the Nag Hammadi story. An
extraordinary series of mishaps plagued scholars' efforts to get
at the bulk of the manuscripts—Egypt's internal political up-
heaval and wars with Israel, scholarly rivalries, and slow progress
in photographing pages at Cairo's Coptic Museum, where most
of the manuscripts are stored.

Part of the excitement over the Dead Sea Scrolls was stimu-
lated by the discovery of ancient biblical manuscripts accompa-
nying the Essene literature—something that the Gnostic library

lacks. But, there were other differences suggesting why the one captured scholarly and public imagination and the other did not.

Some early speculation about the scrolls asked whether Jesus had been an Essene, possibly even the unnamed "righteous teacher" mentioned in the scrolls. But later scholarship discounted both suggestions, leaving only more indirect comparisons to be drawn between the withdrawn Essenes of the Qumran desert community and the early Jesus movement.

Specialists looking for new clues to the life of Jesus and the early church knew by the mid-1950s that the Nag Hammadi Gnostic library contained a large amount of Christian lore ranging from outright heretical writings to near-orthodox philosophical speculations and apocryphal stories. The library also contained *The Gospel of Thomas*, a remarkable arrangement of more than one hundred "sayings of Jesus." This text, one of the few translated and published by 1960, prompted curiosity about a "fifth gospel." The potential for wide religious interest may have been cut short by initial critiques that tended to characterize *Thomas* as a Gnostic compilation derived from Mark, Matthew, and Luke.

The speedier public debut of the Essenes (though not all the scrolls were published even by the late 1980s) has been explained in other ways too. For example, Israel's government supported the scholars involved, perhaps seeing the political benefits as well as the cultural. Egypt, on the other hand, was in the process of great change, at times experiencing damaged relations with the Western countries most of the interested scholars were coming from. Finally, many documents remained in private hands for years.

Scholarly interest in the Nag Hammadi library could not be discouraged indefinitely. The collection—actually containing a variety of religious and philosophical treatises not all "Gnostic"— dates from a period in which much of Western civilization's views of humanity and morality were shaped.

But can today's Christian-influenced culture find any value in the writings of so-called heretics? The Christian church owes much to the Gnostics, religious scholars say. Without the challenge of Gnostic speculation in theology, it would have taken

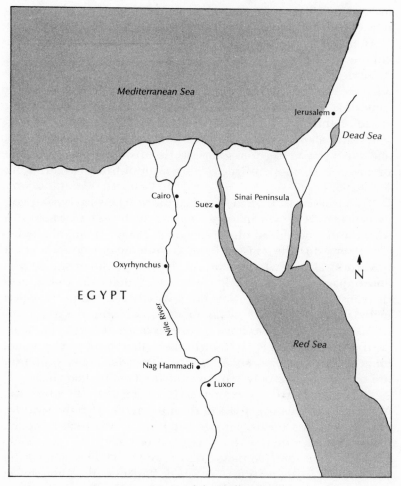

Upper Egypt and the Mediterranean

longer for the church to form creeds, to select the books to be included in the New Testament, and to give authority to bishops.

The Gnostics sometimes have been credited with producing or provoking the first theological works. "They kept alive the great issues of freedom, redemption and grace, which, after the times of Paul and John, were not adequately discussed by second-century Christian writers," says Robert M. Grant.

At the same time, there was a caustic, bitter strain basic to Gnostic thought. "Gnosticism was the religion that expressed most clearly the mood of defeatism and despair that swept the ancient world in the early centuries of the Christian era," says James M. Robinson of the Claremont Graduate School. A foretaste of this mood was seen in the Dead Sea Scrolls. The Essenes' apocalyptic writings showed how a people "that had again and again lost its freedom to one world prove after another gave up any realistic hope of succeeding in the world," according to Robinson.

"Qumran led in part to Nag Hammadi," he writes, referring especially to religious imagery. "Essene dualism condemned this world with its children of darkness and heralded an apocalyptic deliverance for the sons of light; Gnostic mythology portrayed this world as an evil god's prison for the sparks of the divine, and imparted the knowledge with which they could escape to their lost origin above." This otherworldly escapism was halted in Judaism by orthodox rabbis about 100 C.E., but the trend was not erased from Christianity until two or three centuries later. A Gnostic-like religion, Manichaeism, flourished for a while longer, then faded. A small group of Mandeans living in Iraq are considered the only remnants of the Gnostic faith today.

The picture of Gnosticism that had been shaped before the Nag Hammadi discovery was derived primarily from the writings of the second-, third-, and fourth-century Christian leaders. These church fathers wrote polemical pieces against the Gnostics. And even the Neo-platonic philosopher Plotinus joined the anti-Gnostic battle with a work titled, "Against the Gnostics, or Against Those Who Say That the Creator of the World Is Evil and That the World Is Bad." As Plotinus suggested, the Gnostics had little good to say about the here and now, while Greek philosophy taught that the world reflected order and truth.

The Gnostic myth said that truth and knowledge, often symbolically represented by "light," were linked with a higher God. The lower Creator God and his despoiled world were worthless, and a knowledge of this distinction was the first step toward salvation. The church fathers contended that this attitude led the Gnostics toward amoral behavior in the belief that nothing you do in *this* world matters.

The biblical commandment forbidding the coveting of another's wife was considered "laughable" by the leader of the Carpocratian Gnostics, according to Clement of Alexandria. This sect argued that the Creator God gave men their natural sexual urge toward females, yet commanded each man to keep to his own wife. In the light of this "inconsistency," the Carpocratian men and women would conduct feasts, extinguish the light, and "unite as they will and with whom they will." After they exercised themselves in fellowship in such a "love-feast," Clement continued sarcastically, the men demanded sexual submission from the women by day in keeping with the belief they all belong to one another.

The founder of the Gnostic heresies, or so believed the church fathers, was Simon Magus of Samaria. One of those writing of him, about 140 C.E., was Justin Martyr, himself a Samaritan. Justin said that Simon was from the Samaritan village of Gitta, that he demonstrated magical powers, and that he was worshiped as a god.

This Simon was perhaps the magician described in the New Testament book of Acts (8:9–11):

But there was a man named Simon who had previously practiced magic in the city and amazed the nation of Samaria, saying that he himself was somebody great. They all gave heed to him, from the least to the greatest, saying, "This man is that power of God which is called Great." And they gave heed to him, because for a long time he had amazed them with his magic.

However, Acts goes on to say that when the apostle Philip came to preach in Samaria, many people believed and were baptized. "Even Simon himself believed, and after being baptized he continued with Philip. And seeing signs and great miracles performed, he [Simon] was amazed" (Acts 8:13).

The church fathers did not describe the Gnostic Simon as a Christian convert, but as one of history's most outrageous god-pretenders. "He led about with him a certain Helena, whom he had redeemed as a harlot in Tyre, a city of Phoenicia," wrote Irenaeus in the late second century. "She was his first 'thought,' the mother of all, through whom in the beginning he had conceived the idea of making angels and archangels." This "thought" leaped forward from Simon in his earlier existence as the God of the heavens. She gave birth to the angels and worldly powers, which in turn made the world, but those forces detained her because they did not want to be considered merely the products of another being.

Denied her return to her father and suffering under the powers and angels, "she was shut up in a human body and through the centuries, as from one vessel to another, migrated into ever different female bodies," Irenaeus continued. She was in Helen of Troy, for whom the Trojan War was fought, and continued her ignominious travels from body to body until she ended up in a brothel.

At this point, Simon descended to earth as a man to free his errant "thought" and take her to himself. But since the angels were governing the world badly, he decided to bring things into order. Those humans who recognized Simon as God and who acknowledged Helena as the embodiment of his divine thought were extended "redemption," that is, freedom from the enslaving commandments of those who created the world. In reality, Irenaeus claimed, Simon's mystery priests lived immorally, practicing exorcisms and erotic magic and concocting love potions.

Simon's pretensions as God led to his eventual downfall, if the account of another church father, Hippolytus, is right. "[Simon] said that if he were buried alive he would rise again on the third day," Hippolytus wrote. "Commanding a grave to be dug, he ordered his disciples to heap earth upon him. They did as he commanded, but he remained [in it] until this day. For he was not the Christ."

The image of the Gnostics through the ages has not been entirely one of orgy-justifying mystics. Some Gnostic teachings indicated that their abhorrence for the world led to another reaction—withdrawal from society with its corrupting lusts and greeds. Gnosticism, it has been suggested, encouraged lustful abandon on the one hand and asceticism on the other.

Nevertheless, not all Gnostics felt compelled to live in a radical style. One of the few lengthy Gnostic writings that was preserved by church fathers—and one of the most lucid—is a letter to

Flora, apparently a Gnostic initiate, from Ptolemaeus, a Christian Gnostic who frequently quoted Scripture to make his points. He was not willing to condemn the Creator God and conceded that this lower God of the Hebrews was concerned with justice. Ptolemaeus also interpreted the Ten Commandments as pointing toward a reasonable and righteous middle way—neither lustful nor ascetic.

For additional writings by the Gnostics themselves, history had provided little to work with. The British Museum in 1785 acquired manuscripts in Coptic that contained two *Books of Pistis Sophia*. Two Coptic Gnostic *Books of Jeu* were bought near the ancient Egyptian city of Thebes in 1769 but not recognized for their significance until the late 1800s. These writings, according to Hans Jonas, author of *The Gnostic Religion*, represent "a rather low and degenerate level of gnostic thought" belonging to the declining stage of their speculations.

In reconstructing models of Gnostic belief systems, scholars also examined strains in the surviving manuscripts of the Manichaean religion founded by a religious leader named Mani (216–ca. 275 C.E.). Further information was gleaned from old texts of the Mandean sect, from the Egyptian-Greek pagan treatise *Poimandres*, and from some Christian apocryphal writings such as *The Acts of Thomas* that were said to contain Gnostic sections.

Some promise of help came in 1896 when a Coptic codex was purchased in Cairo for the Berlin Museum. It included four Gnostic documents. Unfortunately, these materials still were unpublished by the time of the Nag Hammadi find.

The bulk of the Nag Hammadi texts did not start to become generally available until the mid-1970s. By that time, the significance of the library began to emerge and the origin of Gnostic thought was not such a mystery. Of all the possible religious influences, it appears that the oldest compositions betray an intellectual revolt with Judaism as the starting point. Rabbinic-like commentaries found in some texts treat the God of Judaism with virulent sarcasm. Analysis of these texts, which have little or no Christian influences, permitted some scholars to date them into the first century C.E.—contemporary with the formation of another breakaway from Judaism, Christianity.

Church definitions depict Christian Gnostic heresies as complete distortions of the true teachings of Jesus and his successors. The leading edge of mainstream critical biblical scholarship, however, has disputed the idea that it is as simple as that. Rather, these scholars have said the views of Jesus espoused by what became the orthodox churches triumphed over the views of "losers" in ecclesiastical struggles. The New Testament is a collection of books approved by the "winners," although the Gospels and many epistles received wide acceptance within decades after they were written.

Some Nag Hammadi writings indeed reveal a reactionary stance toward orthodox doctrine, such as the Christian assertion that Jesus suffered on the cross as any mortal would. In that sense, some texts could be called Gnostic "distortions" of what we now call Christian beliefs. This is the Jesus of heresy.

Nevertheless, because Gnostic thought extends back to a period contemporaneous with formative Christianity, researchers have expected more than secondary, heretical ramblings—and they have found it. Without getting ahead of our story, these discoveries tell us more about the Jesus of myth and the Jesus of history:

The Gospel of John, in contrast to other New Testament Gospels, poetically glorifies Jesus as a preexisting heavenly redeemer who descended to spread saving knowledge, then reascended to heaven. Those images may have had a non-Christian inspiration. The same kind of redeemer tale is found in certain Nag Hammadi texts, and some scholars have contended that similar texts influenced John.

A few Nag Hammadi books containing dialogues of the resurrected Jesus with disciples and one book, *The Gospel of Thomas*, and its assemblage of Jesus sayings, are witnesses to the very early emphasis on Jesus' words. Unlike the New Testament Gospels, they never call Jesus the Messiah or Christ, and they do not describe his deeds or death. Scholars studying these works along with other longer-known apocryphal writings are plumbing into a layer of the Jesus tradition sometimes deemed earlier than the New Testament Gospels, which date from the last third of the first century.

The Gnostic manuscripts, it must be said, are read only with difficulty by the uninitiated. Of course, it was meant to be that way in some cases. Some of the writings were labeled "secret books" or "revelations."

In sum, the Nag Hammadi library that made its way to Cairo contained fifty-two whole or partial titles in thirteen books, or codices. Some duplicates were found, so there were forty-six different writings. Of those, forty were previously lost to history except for small fragments of three of them.

Although they were found in 1945, the manuscripts eluded history for another couple of decades. The difficulties in bringing the secret books to public light bedeviled a large cast of characters. The story is best told around a Frenchman who was one of the first to recognize the significance of the find and an American who doggedly completed the task of making the manuscripts available to all.

I. THE DISCOVERY

1. From a Museum Drawer . . .

A young French graduate student arrived in Cairo in September 1947, excited about examining firsthand the vestiges of ancient Christian monastic life in Egypt. While studying and lecturing in Paris, Jean Doresse had steeped himself in the languages and history of this period. And now the French Institute of Archaeology at Cairo had invited him to spend three months exploring for Christian remains in an area three hundred miles south of Cairo in Upper Egypt.

Christianity had put down some of its strongest, earliest roots in Egypt long before the arrival in the seventh century of Islam. Church leaders in Alexandria were voices to contend with as the Christian church developed in the Mediterranean world of the late Roman Empire. The first series of monasteries in the history of Christendom was begun early in the fourth century by monks under St. Pachomius. Born and raised a pagan, Pachomius was said to have become a disciple of the aged hermit Palemon around 315 to 320 C.E. Individual Christian hermits were not uncommon then in Egypt. One of the most popular monks of that period was the venerated St. Anthony.

However, Pachomius eventually sought an alternate style by gathering around him others to form Christian communities along the northern shores of a big bend in the Nile River, which begins north of Luxor and completes its swerve near Nag Hammadi. Innumerable monasteries and convents were started under the influence of Pachomius and his disciples in Egypt. Pachomius's monastic rules later shaped the formation of other religious orders in Christendom.

At first, Jean Doresse's plan to visit the ruins of those monasteries was frustrated. An epidemic of cholera had just hit Egypt that autumn of 1947. Nearly five thousand lives were reported lost in the first month of the disease's spread, mostly in the Nile delta region. Government health measures forced the eager Parisian to postpone his trip to Upper Egypt.

But all was not lost for the slender Frenchman, thirty years old, and his wife, Marianne, who accompanied him. While in Cairo, they had planned to visit the Coptic Museum, a repository of relics from the Coptic period of Egypt. Doresse's wife had known the director of the museum while both were studying in Paris at the École des Hautes Études. Doresse studied Egyptology two years later at the same school and knew of the director's reputation from Marianne and from his professors.

Before leaving Marseilles on September 20 for Egypt, "I wrote and received the most friendly answer," Doresse later recalled. "He was anxious to see me but he would not write why. Arriving in Cairo, we went immediately to the Coptic Museum."

Entering the oldest section of the Egyptian capital, they passed by the ruins of a huge tower, part of the remains of a Roman fortified enclosure. A considerable amount of Christian lore is associated with Old Cairo, including the legend that a church there sits on a spot where the infant Jesus was taken by his parents (in an expansion of the nativity story by Matthew). This is also said to be where the apostle Mark founded the first Christian church in Egypt.

The Coptic Museum, in contrast to its surroundings, has a contemporary look. The entrance of the yellow stucco building leads to a pleasant enclosed courtyard enhanced by marble columns and statues. According to scholars who visited there in later years, tourists are directed to the left where two floors of artifacts are gathered into a seemingly endless display of cloth, papyrus, statuary, jewelry, paintings—nearly all relics from the culture of Egyptian Christians who are known as the Copts.

The Coptic language was developed by Egyptians around the second century C.E., using the alphabet of the widely known Greek language and adding six letters for sounds not found in Greek. Although Coptic was gradually replaced by Arabic as the common tongue in Egypt between the eighth and tenth centuries, the language was preserved in the liturgy of the Coptic Christian church just as Latin continued up to modern times as the liturgical language of the Roman Catholic church. By 1947, the year the Doresses visited Cairo, Coptic was still spoken by some families in the Coptic Christian communities, which made up about 8 percent of the Egyptian population.

To the right of the museum's entrance was a wing containing a large reading room with relatively few books. Doresse and his wife headed to the museum office where they met the director, Togo Mina. A dark-complexioned man of forty-one, Mina was about five feet five inches, and his slightly stooped shoulders only emphasized the difference in height between him and Doresse, who was five feet eleven inches. The two men were only eleven years apart in age, but Mina, who suffered from diabetes and other complications, looked much older.

Mina wasted no time in revealing why he was so interested in Doresse's visit to Cairo. "He opened a drawer of his desk, took out of it a voluminous packet, and showed me, in a bookcover of soft leather, some pages of papyrus filled with large fine Coptic writing." Mina suggested that the documents might date from the third or fourth century C.E.

"He asked me if I could identify the contents of the pages," Doresse said. "From the first few words, I could see that these were Gnostic texts."

One manuscript bore two titles, *The Sacred Book of the Great Invisible Spirit* and *The Gospel of the Egyptians*. This great invisible spirit was described in an opening line as the "Father whose name cannot be uttered," one who came forth from the heights of perfection. The neatly written, ragged-edged text may not have named the unnameable Spirit-Father, but it went on to identify all sorts of other "powers" and "lights" of the heavens.

The packet's first text was a "secret book" of John, *The Apocryphon of John*. The text purported to be the apostle John's account of an appearance by Jesus after his resurrection. After descending as a blazing light from the parted heavens, Jesus told John not only about the array of heavenly powers but also about human origins in a bizarre Gnostic version of the Genesis story.

Doresse warmly congratulated Mina on the extraordinary discovery. Altogether the packet contained five treatises. Besides *The Apocryphon of John* and *The Gospel of the Egyptians*, there was *The Dialogue of the Savior*, in which Jesus answered questions from his disciples as well as from a Mary.

Two other texts resembled each other—*Eugnostos, the Blessed*, basically a non-Christian work in the form of a letter, and *The Sophia of Jesus Christ*, a dialogue between Jesus and his disciples.

Togo Mina (left) and Jean Doresse study the manuscripts at the Coptic Museum. The Museum director and the Frenchman eventually located two other collections from the Nag Hammadi cache in Cairo but were unable to obtain them before Mina died in 1949. Photo courtesy of The Institute for Antiquity and Christianity.

Unlike Mary, Sophia was not another woman follower of Jesus. Sophia is the Greek term for "wisdom," one of many words the scribes did not translate into Coptic.

Curious about how the Coptic Museum acquired these precious writings, Doresse pressed Mina for details. The museum director told him that in the previous year a man showed the papyrus manuscripts to Georgy Sobhy, a museum board member who was trying to popularize the use of Coptic language in Egyptian Christian circles. Sobhy sent the man to Togo Mina, who bought the texts for a reportedly modest price on October 4, 1946, nearly a year before the young Frenchman's visit.

This batch of centuries-old literature, in surprisingly good condition, suddenly opened new doors on the enigmatic Gnostics. Oddly enough, two of the texts Doresse read were not the first copies to be discovered.

The Apocryphon of John and *The Sophia of Jesus Christ* were among four Coptic papyrus texts found in Egypt in 1896 but more than fifty years later were still not published. A noted German professor Carl Schmidt had drawn attention to the find. Excerpts from those writings, which also included the Gnostic *Gospel of Mary* and the Christian apocryphal writing *The Acts of Peter*, appeared in articles around the turn of the century. But full publication of the translations was thwarted in 1912 when a water pipe burst in the printer's cellar and ruined the plates. Schmidt returned to the work periodically and was preparing a new edition from the old proofs shortly before his death in 1938. During World War II the task was eventually entrusted to Walter C. Till, an Austrian scholar.

Now, in the Cairo of 1947, a new cache of Coptic Gnostic scripture surfaced, and Doresse had to reflect on the possibility that his copies of *The Apocryphon of John* and *The Sophia of Jesus Christ* could beat the Till versions into print. It was time for co-operation, however, not one-upmanship. Doresse and Mina decided to invite three other people to participate in publishing translations of the Coptic Museum's texts. They were Canon Etienne Drioton, the French director general of the Egyptian Department of Antiquities; Henri-Charles Puech of Paris, Doresse's teacher and a professor of the history of religions, and Till. Both Till and Doresse would benefit from comparisons of their duplicate texts, noting the differences in footnotes to their respective translations, but as it turned out Doresse's plans went unfulfilled.

2. Cairo, Luxor, Jerusalem, and New York

A few days after Doresse had examined the remarkable packet in the director's desk drawer, Mina asked Doresse if he would like to see more papyrus pages similar to those they had studied at the museum. These, Mina said, were held by Albert Eid, a Belgian antiquities dealer in Cairo.

Doresse responded eagerly, and the two men jumped into Mina's car, Mina switching to the dark-tinted glasses he always wore when driving. Eid's shop was in a section called Khan Khalil.

"Eid was good enough to let me look at the manuscripts he had bought," Doresse said. In appearance and content they resembled the museum's papyri, though these pages were in poorer condition. They were "undoubtedly Gnostic," Doresse concluded. The Frenchman found, among other texts, *The Gospel of Truth* and a letterlike treatise about the resurrection addressed to a Rheginos.

Mina and Doresse left Eid's shop determined to find out where these two sets of manuscripts had been discovered in the hope that yet more could be found at the source. But inquiries along the antiquities grapevine yielded little. "They spoke mysteriously of a large find of manuscripts having been made near a hamlet called Hamra-Dum, well to the north of Luxor," Doresse said.

Mina and the Doresses went to Eid's shop again, and Mina told the dealer that the Coptic Museum wanted to buy the manuscripts for a reasonable price. Mina warned Eid he could not allow the documents to leave Egypt. The Belgian agreed to supply Doresse with photographs of the fragile papyrus leaves; if the pages left the country or somehow disappeared, the photos were to be handed over at no cost to the Coptic Museum.

The ruins of the Basilica of St. Pachomius appear in the foreground. Doresse originally planned to study the vestiges of the first Christian monastic communities in the region of the Nile. His realization that Gnostic manuscripts were discovered in this region led him there for another reason. Photo courtesy of The Institute for Antiquity and Christianity.

In the course of their dealings, Eid told Mina and Doresse of the possibility that still more codices—a technical name for the leather-bound "books" of papyri—could be found in Cairo. But Eid could not prove it, said Doresse, "so Togo thought that it was one more legend of fabulous discoveries aimed at increasing the price of Eid's codex."

Despite the sketchiness of the rumor about the Gnostic codices being found near a hamlet in Upper Egypt, Doresse felt it was worth checking. Hamrah Dum was located in the very area that was the object of Doresse's original mission to Egypt. He reached Upper Egypt by plane, the railway service still being suspended because of the cholera epidemic.

Hoping to hear stories of a large papyrus discovery, Doresse spent long hours rambling over ruins of Coptic monasteries and remains of earlier Egyptian greatness, the monuments of the pharaohs. To inquire openly about such a discovery would have invited financial suspension on any items still circulating. "The silence that invariably hides the real circumstances surrounding great finds—and which we had thought we might break—was again impenetrable," he said.

Unknown to Doresse or Mina, or to the rest of the world, about the same time in Jerusalem the significance of another amazing discovery was coming to light. A portion of the now-famous Dead Sea Scrolls had been taken to Jerusalem and Bethlehem by Bedouin tribesmen who had discovered them in caves and sold them to antiquities dealers. It wasn't until November 24, 1947, that the value of the scrolls was recognized. That moment came when archeologist Elazar L. Sukenik of Hebrew University peered through a barbed-wire barrier at an inscribed scrap of leather from one of the scrolls and sensed their antiquity. Tension was high then in Palestine because any day the United Nations was expected to vote on the establishment of a Jewish state. Sections of Jerusalem were divided to keep Arabs and Jews apart, but Sukenik obtained military pass to keep an appointment to see some scroll fragments.

On November 29, Sukenik and an Armenian friend made a bus trip to Bethlehem to purchase three scrolls; then they rode back to Jerusalem with the scrolls wrapped in paper under their arms. "All around were groups of Arabs, some sullen and silent, others gesticulating wildly," Sukenik wrote in a personal journal. That night the news came that the United Nations had voted to establish Israel, and the predicted protests by groups of Palestinians began.

Months earlier, four other scrolls had come into the possession of a Syrian Orthodox church leader in Jerusalem Mar Athanasius Y. Samuel. It was not long before Sukenik and Americans William Brownlee and John Trever were in contact with the prelate. Thus began the story of the Dead Sea Scrolls, which in time would be identified as the sacred writings and Bible texts of a Jewish sect called the Essenes.

Like the scrolls, the Coptic Gnostic codices had been discovered earlier by people unaware of their significance. In both cases, it wasn't until the fall of 1947 that a scholar would start the necessary backtracking to find the sources.

Unsuccessful in his trip to the Luxor region, Doresse returned to Cairo in December, only a short time before his three-month mission was to end. "Togo Mina was now definitely persuaded that there was nothing more to be discovered," Doresse said. An announcement of the museum's acquisition was given to the Egyptian press, and Cairo newspapers of January 11 and 12, 1948, carried brief items on the discovery. The news prompted "no great stir in a country so inured to archeological marvels," said Doresse.

Back in Paris, Doresse got together with his professor, Henri-Charles Puech, to write a report for the scholarly world. It was forwarded on February 8 to the prestigious Académie des Inscriptions et Belles-Lettres. Doresse's summary account to the academy, to which Peuch "lent his authority," as Doresse put it, aroused a "moderate" degree of interest. *Le Monde,* a leading French newspaper, ran a three-sentence story on February 23 under the headline, "Discovery of a Papyrus of the Fourth Century":

The Academy has been informed of the discovery, recently made in Egypt, of a collection on papyrus, of 152 pages, dating from the sixth [*sic*] century of our era. It contains in Coptic translation five unpublished Gnostic books. They furnish interesting information about the beliefs of that time.

Although the news article spoke of only five Gnostic books, Doresse had also mentioned in his academy report the existence of the Eid codex which contained another (forty leaves (80 pages of writing). That was nowhere near the total number of manuscripts that would turn up.

Several months into 1948 Doresse received from Cairo some mail with photographs of yet more Coptic texts on papyrus, again Gnostic in content. He appealed for travel funds from the secretary general of the academy and obtained the money in short order.

Arriving in Cairo in October, Doresse met with Maria Dattari, whose father was a noted coin collector. Miss Dattari, in sending the photographs to Paris, had indicated that she was the owner, but representing her in Cairo was Phocion J. Tano, an antiquities dealer who claimed to be her business manager.

Doresse had met Tano before he left Egypt at the end of 1947. Tano advised him to stay longer then because of indications that more manuscripts were around. Sitting down to scan the Dattari-Tano codices, Doresse found himself before hundreds of papyrus pages held together in the now-familiar soft leather bindings. "I was allowed to make no more than a rapid inspection of them," Doresse. Air raid warnings, which blared at what seemed to Doresse to be the slightest provocation, cut short the few evenings he was permitted to peruse the pages. Egypt had been at war with Israel off and on since May 15, when the Jewish state had officially come into being.

Enthralled by the magnitude of the Dattari-Tano codices, Doresse ran his eyes and fingers over four times as many Gnostic texts as he had already been privileged to see, most of the treatises never before available to historians. It was later determined that Tano had eight codices and parts from four others.

"I went . . . from surprise to astonishment," recalled Doresse. He encountered some "sensationally attractive titles," such as *The Revelation of Adam to His Son Seth* (later named simply *The Apocalypse of Adam*), *The Letter of Peter to Philip*, *The Gospel of Philip*, and *The Gospel of Thomas*. The gospels attributed to Philip and Thomas were unlike the four New Testament Gospels since they did not concern themselves with a narrative of the life and death of Jesus. *The Gospel of Philip* appeared to Doresse to be a rambling treatise consisting of "lofty speculations." *The Gospel of Thomas* strung together seemingly unconnected sayings of Jesus. It began:

These are the secret sayings which the living Jesus spoke and which Didymos Judas Thomas wrote down.

And he said, "Whoever finds the interpretation of these sayings will not experience death."

Jesus said, "Let him who seeks continue seeking until he finds. When he finds, he will become troubled. When he becomes troubled, he will be astonished, and he will rule over the all."

Doresse could see that penetrating the meaning of the sayings would be difficult in light of the cryptic nature of many passages. Nonetheless, much of *Thomas* went over familiar ground— parables about the lost sheep and the mustard seed, proverbs about the blind following the blind and new wine in old wine-skins. The *Thomas* versions nearly always varied a bit from the parallels in Mark, Matthew, or Luke, but then even the New Testament Gospels differed among themselves.

In writing about the manuscript discoveries about a decade later, Doresse predicted that *Thomas* would be "indispensable" for critical work on passages in the canonical Gospels and also on sayings that the canonical Gospels "ignored." In the latter category is a Jesus saying that had been known previously only from the writings of the Alexandrian church father Origen: "He who is near me is near the fire, and he who is far from me is far from the kingdom" (saying no. 82 in *Thomas*).

Even in 1948, Puech, Doresse's mentor, realized that the discovery of *Thomas* in a full, Coptic version ended the mystery about the identification of some papyrus fragments found in Egypt at the ancient Greco-Roman site of Oxyrhynchus before the turn of the twentieth century. The three fragments, each written in Greek, roughly matched the wording in three different sections of the Coptic version of *The Gospel of Thomas*.

Doresse undoubtedly could have captured worldwide attention by announcing the discovery of a "fifth Gospel," but common sense and ordinary scruples were enough to encourage him to proceed with quiet care. Such an announcement would have put the manuscripts out of reach financially for the Coptic Museum or any reputable scholarly agency and would have prolonged the opportunity to translate them. Announcing another Gospel would be meaningless without a decent description of its contents, something that Doresse had no chance to give as yet.

Scholars know only too well that careful study and comparisons with similar documents can produce unforeseen results. The Gnostic library was too large to say immediately that *The Gospel of Thomas* would be the only book pertinent to Christian origins to emerge from the collection.

Mina and Doresse began the touchy matter of negotiating to buy the Dattari-Tano collection. The situation was sensitive because the Egyptian government then had a tendency to take the legal expedient of confiscating historical treasures rather than paying a fair price, said Doresse. The practice was so common that few owners of a valuable antiquity, however legitimately acquired, offered it to the government. They preferred instead to export it and sell it on the clandestine market.

Mina secured the promise of some government funds, but bargaining with the Dattari-Tano team was postponed when political unrest in Cairo brought national affairs to a halt. Prime Minister Nokrashi Pasha was assassinated on December 28, 1948, by a member of the Moslem Brotherhood, a group Pasha had ordered suppressed the month before. The Coptic Museum would have to await the formation of a new government.

That wasn't the first setback of the winter of 1948-1949. Another set of Gnostic texts slipped from the museum's grasp.

Eid had taken his papyri to New York City, looking for a market. The Belgian antiquities dealer earlier bragged to Doresse and Mina that he planned to smuggle out the Gnostic pages, claiming the administrative controls on export of antiquities then "were completely inefficient." When leaving the country, Eid showed the Antiquities Department an assortment of carved figures, coins, manuscripts, and other items he planned to sell in the United States—nothing Egyptian authorities would insist on keeping in the country, according to Doresse. Eid may have figured a way to slip the Gnostic papyri into a box at the last minute before it was nailed shut by the authorities, conjectured Doresse. "Anyway, he told everyone afterward that the thing was so easy to do!" said Doresse.

Eid had written to the University of Michigan library, known for its papyrus collections, in the winter of 1946–1947. Library officials declined to buy, saying that Eid's asking price of $20,000 was too high. Now in New York City in January 1949, with *The Gospel of Truth* and other texts in hand, Eid contacted the university through an agent, saying he was willing to settle for $10,000. Though the university was advised of the documents' importance, officials decided not to resume their collection of manuscripts.

Eid then offered the papyri to the Bollingen Foundation in New York for $12,000. Established by philanthropist Paul Mellon, the Bollingen Foundation had been organized to publish specialized academic books in such fields as comparative religion, mythology, philosophy, and archeology. However, Jack D. Barrett, a Bollingen official, told Eid that the foundation did not normally buy ancient manuscripts. Even Eid's request to keep the manuscripts in the foundation's safe was turned down. Frustrated, the antiquities dealer departed for Brussels, where he put his pages in a safety deposit box.

The connection between Eid and the Bollingen Foundation was instigated by Gilles Quispel, a thirty-two-year-old Dutch schoolteacher with training in early church history. Quispel had been studying about the second-century Gnostic thinker Valentinus when he read of Doresse's reports on the Gnostic papyri in the spring of 1948. Quispel was later able to question Doresse in person about the possible Valentinian content of Eid's codex. That summer Quispel urged the New York foundation to buy the writings if they became available and gave Eid, through Doresse, the foundation's address.

But after Eid's abortive trip to the United States, Quispel lost track of Eid. Quispel was in touch with Puech, and both wanted to acquire a buyer to permit them to do a scholarly treatment of the work, but they hoped to keep Doresse off the team. "The situation was extremely delicate," Quispel said. "The rumor went round—which later turned out to be true—that its owner had died. It was not known where the codex was to be found." After rejoining his wife, Simone, in Cairo, Eid died in the winter of 1950–51.

Meanwhile, precautions had been taken in Cairo to safeguard the texts owned by Miss Dattari and Tano. One report said that an Italian woman, Miss Dattari, was stopped at the Cairo airport attempting to take most of the manuscripts to Rome with the intent of presenting them to the pope. The government's minister of education told her she could not export them, and he offered her 300 Egyptian pounds apiece for the eight codices. She refused.

Egyptian officials decided to confiscate the collection, telling the owners that after Doresse made an inventory of the books money would be raised for the purchase. A new government formed in February 1949 and it looked for a while that Tano and Miss Dattari would get a fair price. The education ministry was about to allocate 40,000 to 50,000 pounds when that government also fell on July 25.

The bulk of the Nag Hammadi library had been placed un-

The bulk of the Nag Hammadi Gnostic library is shown here! Eleven of the thirteen codices had leather covers. They are among the earliest examples of bound books ever found. Photo courtesy of The Institute for Antiquity and Christianity.

ceremoniously in a suitcase by the Department of Antiquities, indicative of the feeling that this was merely a temporary action. The documents sat in the suitcase for the next seven years! It was opened only after the texts were declared national property and the owners' lawsuit failed.

3. The Jesus Curse

The repeated disappointments in 1949 were taking their toll on the museum director. Sick for several months, Mina died in October at the age of forty-three. Doresse was convinced that the delays contributed to his death. He recalled Mina's "anguish" one day when it was learned that the government was postponing an important decision.

The demise of Mina . . . the disappearance of one set of manuscripts from Europe . . . a suitcase of papyrus texts sealed by government inaction in Cairo—all these were misfortunes and obstacles to revealing what the Gnostics considered to be their sacred secrets. The events prompted Doresse to wonder: were commercial and academic covetousness and political instability the only deterrents? Could the troubles be due instead to the "maledictions that the Egyptian Gnostics had written out in full upon their works against anyone gaining unlawful knowledge of them"?

Several Gnostic works described themselves as "secret" and "hidden" mysteries, but *The Apocryphon of John* contained a specific warning of a "curse." Near the text's conclusion, the savior (Jesus) tells John to write his teachings down and put them in a safe place. Then Jesus said: "Cursed be everyone who will exchange these things for a gift, or for food, or for drink, or for clothing, or for any other such thing." This malediction, of course, appears also at the end of the Berlin Museum's copy of the *Apocryphon*, which had defied publication for a half century.

Doresse was aware in his musings that Upper Egypt, reputedly the area where the Gnostic manuscripts were found, was the focus of public fascination in the 1920s and 1930s over the so-called pharaoh's curse. The tomb of King Tutankhamen, who died before 1300 B.C.E., was discovered in 1922 across the Nile River from Luxor. The tomb's remarkable secret compartments, each yielding gold and silver treasures, generated enormous worldwide curiosity. During a three-month period in 1926, an estimated 12,300 tourists visited the tomb in the Valley of the Kings where a series of pharaonic tombs had been found over the years.

But during the decade following the unsealing of the tomb of King Tut, as he became popularly known, more than twenty persons said to be connected with that expedition died. The first such "victim" was Lord Carnarvon, the supervisor of the excavation, who died April 6, 1923, after three weeks' illness precipitated by a mosquito bite. News reports later heralded the "third victim," the "fourth victim," and so on. Some deaths appeared to be quite unusual; others were rather unremarkable, but talk about the effects of the curse persisted. It was said to have wording such as: "Death will come on swift pinions to those who disturb the rest of the Pharaoh."

By 1933, however, Egyptologists debunked the pharaoh's curse story on at least two points: some "victims" on the lists were entirely unrelated to the tomb expedition, and no such curse was ever found inscribed in or around the tomb.

Howard Carter, the Englishman who was the principal archeologist and discoverer, attributed the speculations on the one hand to a "form of literary amusement" and on the other to "the foolish superstitions which are far too prevalent among emotional people in search of 'psychic' excitement." Carter himself died in London in 1939 at about the age of sixty-six.

Doresse alluded to the Gnostic warning against revealing their secrets in the introduction to his book, *The Secret Books of the Egyptian Gnostics*, published in English in 1960. (By that time, however, some of the Gnostic essays were being published, and the list of deaths had not expanded beyond Eid and Mina.)

The "curse" of Jesus in *The Apocryphon of John*, put into Jesus' mouth by Gnostic authors, followed a time-honored practice of mystic groups warning their members that such sacred scriptures should not fall into the wrong hands. For historians, much more interesting was the advice to put the writings in a safe place. In the case of the Gnostic papyri, the place, wherever it was, had been "safe" for centuries.

Where was the Gnostic library hidden? wondered Doresse. A tomb? Pagan or Christian? In the ruins of a house or monastic

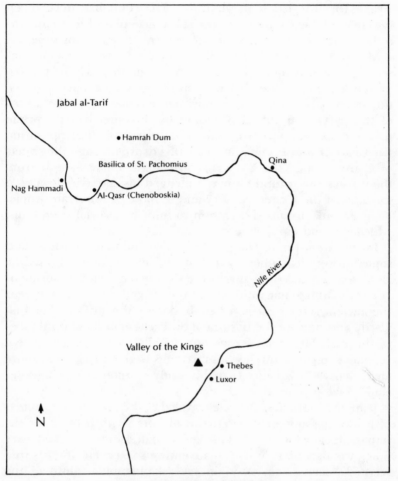

Nag Hammadi and Environs

building? How old were the books? Under what circumstances could they have been buried?

In Israel, by 1949, comparable questions were already being answered about the Dead Sea Scrolls. A cave that had contained some of the scrolls was found sixteen miles east of Jerusalem in cliffs overlooking the Dead Sea. Nearby was Khirbet Qumran,

Arabic for "the ruins of Qumran." The ruins had never been systematically excavated, but the site was explored in 1949. Uncovering the Essene "monastery" was only a matter of time.

Meanwhile, in Egypt the political situation was improving considerably, encouraging Doresse to plan another trip to the rumored location of the Gnostic discoveries. On January 3, 1950, the Wafd party won a big majority in elections, and the leader of the party, Mustafa el Nahas Pasha, became the new prime minister. On January 16, amid widespread political optimism, King Farouk and Prime Minister Pasha drove through the streets of Cairo to open the Egyptian Parliament. In his speech from the throne, the rotund monarch pledged his country's loyalty to the aims of the United Nations and to those of the Arab people. King Farouk promised attention to improved social conditions, education, and employment.

In this atmosphere Doresse left Cairo late that month to find some answers in Upper Egypt. Bits of information collected by Doresse indicated the papyri were discovered near the village of Hamrah Dum. That would place the alleged discovery site near the ancient settlement of Chenoboskia by the cliffs of Jabal al-Tarif. The ruins of the Basilica of St. Pachomius lay several miles to the east, but Doresse was now looking for signs of ancient "enemies" of the church whose writings were bound to tell more about early Christianity than his study of monastery sites ever could have produced.

Jean and Marianne Doresse traveled to the area on the pretext of inspecting any ancient remains of note. With his moustache, pith helmet, white scarf, and sport coat, Doresse looked very much the part of a European adventure seeker. He and his wife feigned "deepest curiosity" in several pharaonic tombs of the Sixth Dynasty located halfway up the eastern face of Jabal al-Tarif. Pillagers had long ago robbed the tombs of any obvious relics. The caves were accessible because rock debris formed slopes halfway up the cliffs at some spots. Approaching the series of caves from the south, the Doresses were shown the first cave known for its wall writings in red paint. They were the beginnings, in Coptic, of Psalms 51 through 93, possibly the writings of a Christian monk. In caves further to the north they were shown Greek invocations to Zeus Sarapis. Below the caves for

Jean Doresse (third from left) and his party of guides who led him to an area at the foot of Jabal al-Tarif (in background) where they said the manuscripts were found. Nag Hammadi is about ten miles southwest of the discovery site. Photo courtesy of The Institute for Antiquity and Christianity.

some two hundred yards lay a strip of barren, sandy ground that, Doresse was told (wrongly apparently), was once a Greco-Roman cemetery.

The European couple was led by the peasant guides "of their own initiative to the southern part of the cemetery and [they] showed us a row of shapeless cavities," said Doresse. In one of these holes, they said, some peasants from Hamrah Dum and environs were digging for nitrate-rich soil called *sabakh* when they found a large jar filled with leaves of papyrus bound together like books. A Coptic priest was later summoned from a nearby village. He tried to read them, but couldn't, being familiar only with the Coptic of his church's liturgy.

Doresse heard a report that some peasants burned a few pages to heat their tea. The peasants, it was also said, divided up the treasure, some selling their portions for a mere 3 Egyptian pounds to middlemen who took them to Cairo in batches to offer on the antiquities market.

Although more details about the discovery would be learned twenty-five years later, there has never been doubt that information about the container was correct. The ancient use of jars to store manuscripts was known. The Dead Sea Scrolls—believed to date from the second century B.C.E. and thereafter—were found in large pottery jars.

Doresse was able to learn only that the jar was found in either 1945 or 1946. Subsequent interviewing of villagers put the time of discovery in December of 1945.

A more difficult dating problem, given the lapse of centuries, was when the manuscripts were hidden. Versed in Coptic Christian history and the monastic beginnings of that region of Egypt, Doresse could piece together the events of the fourth century for a possible answer. The biographies of monastery founder Pachomius, who died about 348, did not mention any struggles with Gnostics. But in 367, Theodorus, one of Pachomius's successors, ordered that a Lenten letter issued by Bishop Athanasius of Alexandria be translated into Coptic and read in all the monasteries. Athanasius's letter listed what were to be the church-recognized books of the Old and New Testaments. In enumerating the canonical books, Athanasius also denounced heretical books that he said were composed to sound as if they were written centuries earlier by the apostles.

This authoritative letter from Alexandria could have provided the opportunity monastic leaders had sought to order the destruction of all unorthodox books. Doresse said that the Theodorus who dictated the wide reading of the letter may have been the same Theodorus who once deplored a heretical book that said that "after Eve was deceived and had eaten the fruit of the tree, it was of the devil that she gave birth to Cain." This comes close to characterizing some passages in *The Apocryphon of John*, a book that appears in three copies in the Gnostic library.

That reconstruction of a possible situation in the late fourth century is hardly conclusive, but other evidence points to that period as well. Dates were found—not in the manuscripts, but on scraps of papyrus stuffed into the covers of the volumes. These scraps, used to stiffen the covers, included receipts and other items bearing dates ranging from 333 to 348 C.E. Thus, the manuscripts were probably bound into book form after 350 and may have been hidden in the jar in 367, or as late as 400.

The stories themselves are older. For one thing, scholars are confident that the treatises were translated from the Greek originals because of the sometimes poor renditions into Coptic of passages that were smoother in the equivalent Greek. Also, Greek was more likely the original language because of its widespread use in the Hellenistic age.

The texts are undoubtedly copies rather than original translations. One scribe noted on a page of papyrus between two treatises: "I have copied this one treatise only, for it was among a great many that have come into my hands." He had not copied others, the scribe added, thinking it would have been burdensome.

Assigning estimated dates of composition to each Gnostic "gospel," "apocryphon," "treatise," and "apocalypse" is more imprecise, even using methods of literary and historical comparison. Some of the writings date at least back into the second century when church father Irenaeus was composing tracts against the Gnostics and cited a Gnostic text similar to *The Apocryphon of John.*

For Doresse, who now had photographs of the tall, rugged Jabal al-Tarif and the probable discovery site, the find was of extraordinary importance for archeological reasons alone—one of the most "voluminous" and "precious" libraries of papyrus writings ever found. Doresse was soon to exult in an illustrated article for the U.S. journal *Archeology:* "The number of codices, the care given to their binding and in particular the ancient techniques of these bindings, and the beauty of the different hands establish it as the most remarkable ancient library we possess; there does not exist, even in Greek papyri, anything comparable." Indeed, these were crafted not long after the invention of the codex, a book form as opposed to the rolled scroll. The leather bindings from the Gnostic library are among the oldest ever to survive.

Though Doresse would attach the ancient place name of Chenoboskion, also spelled Chenoboskia, to the discovery in future references, later scholars linked the library with the nearest modern town of any size, Nag Hammadi.

In fact, during their fruitful January 1950 visit Doresse and his wife had been the guests of the director of a large Nag Hammadi sugar factory. Preparing to leave Nag Hammadi and eager to share the information about the discovery site, Doresse inquired whether there was a faster route back to their camp adjacent to the Valley of the Kings and across the river from Luxor, the major departure point from Upper Egypt. The Doresses had driven to Nag Hammadi in an old canvas-top Italian car built especially for a Mussolini general in World War II and captured by the British. But the route was long (125 miles) and circuitous, following the winding eastern bank of the Nile most of the way.

Employees at the sugar factory told him there was a way to travel to the Valley of the Kings staying always on the western side of the Nile. There was only about ten miles of flat desert to cross at one point where the road ended. "It was then a question not of a full day, but of a few hours to get from Nag Hammadi to our camp," said Doresse. "We started after lunch without haste on the road on the west bank of the Nile."

They picked up a peasant guide at a hamlet near the stretch of desert they had to cross. The guide assured them it was easy to get to the pharaonic temple site of Dandara where the road resumed.

"Yes, it would have been easy with a camel," Doresse recalled, "but the man had no idea of the limited possibilities of a car. We started driving through something comparable to a thoroughly bombed field for one hour before the petrol pump of the car began leaking."

Doresse repaired the pump several times, advancing slowly until darkness made it impossible to fix the leaks. "The pylons of the temple of Dandara were in the distance. We left the car and proceeded on foot, with myself running ahead of my wife and the so-called guide." On the way, Doresse encountered a Bedouin hamlet where a pack of dogs nipped at his trousers, tearing his skin and drawing blood with some bites.

But arriving at the Dandara temple, they found immediate

help from a professor who was encamped there on a project to copy down inscriptions. The next morning, Doresse improvised a makeshift fuel supply to the carburetor, and the car made it easily to their camp.

Since Doresse had no chance to have the dog or dogs that bit him examined for rabies, he had to return to Cairo to begin antirabies injections. Had Doresse taken the "Jesus curse" seriously, he might have associated his bad luck with acquiring information about the hiding place of the Gnostic library.

If Doresse worried, it was not apparent in his later recollection of the episode. He received daily injections of a "medicine which looked like tepid butter" for one month, but the shots did not produce so much pain as exceptional itching. The Rabies Institute in Cairo was "perfectly managed," and in fact Doresse found that Cairo at that time of the year was "an agreeable town with plenty of intellectual, artistic and gastronomical possibilities."

Events moved slowly after the excitement of the early weeks of 1950. A successor to Togo Mina wasn't named until 1951— one Pahor Labib. The suitcase containing the voluminous Dattari-Tano manuscripts was transferred from the Antiquities Department to the Coptic Museum on June 9, 1952, but the luggage remained sealed.

Cairo erupted in political turmoil that summer. Anglo-Egyptian relations had worsened, and nationalist feelings were on the rise. Administration changes by King Farouk never brought lasting satisfaction. A coup d'etat was staged by army officers on the night of July 23, 1952, under the direction of Major General Mohammed Naguib. The group included two colonels who would be future prime ministers, Gamal Abdul Nasser and Anwar Sadat. The new military leaders demanded and got a new regime and the abdication of King Farouk.

The revolution had a sweeping effect on Egyptian institutions. The Department of Antiquities, which had been under French direction since Napoleon's invasion of Egypt, was reorganized. Drioton was dismissed, and an Egyptian director was named in his place.

During all his Gnostic-related adventures in Egypt, Doresse never abandoned his original desire to study vestiges of early Christian monastic life. One of his study trips took him to two

Coptic monasteries in the desert near the Red Sea. The Frenchman was growing increasingly disappointed by the lack of
progress on the manuscripts. His hope to join Puech in a translation team never materialized. Doresse, who lacked a doctorate
then, was at a disadvantage in securing the respect and coop-
eration of the scholars back in Europe. Puech and Quispel en-
listed the help of diplomatic envoys to elicit promises from Eid's
widow to sell her collection to them. The two scholars were worried, however, because Doresse held photographs of the pages,
giving him the right to translate and critique the manuscripts on
his own.

The European-based scholars tried to isolate Doresse. Prints
of the Eid codex, given to the Coptic Museum after the actual
pages had been spirited out of Egypt, somehow disappeared
from the director's office after Mina's death. After he left Egypt
in February 1953 to take an archeological appointment in Ethiopia, Doresse mailed another set of Eid codex photographs to the
museum, "but it seems that it was lost again!" he said. He still
retained another set, but Eid's widow, seeking to make some
money on the codex, had asked Doresse not to publish and he
kept his word.

Many years later Doresse recalled that he fretted little about
the kind of "curse" associated with either King Tut's tomb or
the warning in *The Apocryphon of John*. "As for the difficulties in
1949 and in the following years," said Doresse, "the true 'curses'
were in fact the 'curses' emanating from antique dealers and
from scholars, each of them against his colleagues. If I rather
[preferred] to be far from my discovery, it was due to this kind
of malediction."

4. The Jung Codex

On a Sunday afternoon, November 15, 1953, in Zurich, Switzerland, an announcement was made to the press concerning a set of manuscripts "presented" publicly to the famous seventy-eight-year-old psychoanalyst Carl Gustav Jung. The London *Times* published a six-hundred-word article the next day under the headline, "New Light on a Coptic Codex." The news story, filed by an unnamed correspondent, began:

The contents of a codex of four Coptic Christian writings attributed to the second century A.D., which were acquired last year by the Jung Institute for Analytical Psychology in Zurich, were described at a press conference here this afternoon, when the papyri under the title Codex Jung, were presented to Professor Jung, founder of the institute.

The codex contains a heretical fifth Gospel and it is believed by the institute that the manuscripts will have outstanding importance for the study of early Christian doctrine and relations between Gnosticism, Judaism and Christianity.

The occasion was one of legitimate self-congratulation by the institute because, but for the pertinacity of its experts and the good fortune of finding a financial backer in Switzerland at the right moment, there might have been no Codex Jung here. The long and delicate negotiations to acquire the manuscripts were described by Professor Gilles Quispel, of the University of Utrecht, and Professor H. Puech, of the College de France . . .

The article went on to summarize the find near Nag Hammadi and the institute's acquisition of the codex spirited out of Egypt by Albert Eid. It was claimed that *The Gospel of Truth*—"the heretical fifth gospel"—and two other treatises in the codex were authored by Valentinus, the second-century Gnostic teacher, and his school. Thus did Eid's codex resurface publicly and acquire the name of its famous recipient.

After Quispel lost track of the codex following Eid's death in 1949, efforts were still being made to interest the Bollingen Foundation in buying the papyri should they be relocated. Even

Jung himself wrote to New York, urging the purchase. C. A. Meier of the Jung Institute eventually learned through diplomatic contacts that the codex was sitting in a Brussels safety deposit box. In the summer of 1951 Meier was able to find Simone Eid. The parties agreed at an August meeting that the Bollingen Foundation would be asked to buy the writings. The purchase was dependent on Quispel's examination of the papyri to verify their genuineness and particularly to see of they were Valentinian.

Typical of the slow proceedings, the examination did not occur until seven months later. "Although it was not possible to unpack the papyri," Quispel said, "and such indeed was not justified because of the dilettante way in which they had been packed up, the reading of a single page convinced me that it was Valentinian." Quispel recommended buying them, but Mrs. Eid suddenly asked for a delay, and the New York foundation made some stipulations about furnishing the money that seemed certain to slow matters more. "It appeared as if our exertions spread over four years had all come to nothing," said Quispel.

At that point, Meier decided to phone an American businessman, George H. Page, living near Zurich. Page promised to provide the money—35,000 Swiss francs (the equivalent then of $8,009)—in an act later announced to the press as "one of generosity without parallel in the annals of knowledge."

The purchase was completed on May 10, 1952, when Quispel appeared at a Brussels cafe two hours late because he had missed a train connection. He turned the check over to a middleman and was handed the manuscripts. At the request of Mrs. Eid the transaction was not made public for eighteen months, evidently for financial reasons.

The presentation of the archeological find to a psychoanalyst might have seemed odd to outsiders, but not to admirers of Jung. Jung made a serious study of the Gnostics from 1916 to 1926, attracted by what he saw as the Gnostic writers' confrontations with "the primal world of the unconscious." He ended that ten-year effort with an unrequited feeling, largely because of the paucity of sources. Jung said the Gnostics were too remote in time, without any psychohistorical link to the present. Only subsequently, by his own account, through his study of the mystical alchemists of the Middle Ages did he find what he considered a bridge between Gnosticism and "the modern psychology of the unconscious."

Jung credited Sigmund Freud with introducing the classical Gnostic motif of the wicked paternal authority into contemporary psychology. The evil Creator God of the Gnostics "reappeared in the Freudian myth of the primal father and the gloomy superego deriving from that father," Jung said. "In Freud's myth he became a demon who created a world of disappointments, illusions and suffering."

Missing from Freud's system, Jung said, was another essential aspect of Gnosticism—the primordial feminine spirit from another, yet higher God who gave humans the possibility of spiritual transformation. Writing this shortly after Pope Pius XII issued a 1950 papal bull on the Assumption of the Blessed Virgin Mary, Jung applauded the church for its partial recognition of the feminine aspect of divinity. He said that in effect the bull affirmed that Mary as the Bride is united with the Son in the heavenly bridal chamber, and as Sophia (Wisdom) she is united with the Godhead.

Through their myth making, many Gnostics showed themselves to be "not so much heretics as theologians" or even "psychologists," Jung asserted. For example, Jung said, the position of respect given by some Gnostic groups to the snake was not a strange as one might think. The snake represents the "extra-human quality in man," he said.

Jung found important symbolism in a lurid Christian-Gothic story recounted by fourth-century church father Epiphanius from a Gnostic text called *The Great Questions of Mary* (not found in the Nag Hammadi library). In the story, Jesus is said to have taken Mary onto a mountain where he produced a woman from his side and began to have intercourse with her. Eating his own flowing semen, he said that this was to be done that we might have life.

Mary was so shocked she sank to the ground.

Raising her up, Jesus asked, "Why do you doubt me, O you of little faith?"

Jesus' further remarks were sayings borrowed from the Gospel of John, including, "If I have told you earthly things and you do not believe, how can you believe if I tell you heavenly things?" (John 3:12) and ". . . unless you eat the flesh of the Son of man and drink his blood, you have no life in you" (John 6:53).

Jung said that the mountain represented the place of spiritual ascent and revelation, a well-known mythical motif. Christ was another Adam, who had received his conjugal mate from his side. "Just as Adam, before the creation of Eve, was supposed by various traditions to be male/female, so Christ here demonstrates his androgyny in a drastic way," Jung said.

Taken literally, the story would be as offensive to third- or fourth-century tastes as to those today, Jung wrote. "For the medical psychologist there is nothing very lurid about it," he added, saying that such "shocking" images can appear in dreams or during psychological treatment. By quoting John 3:12, said Jung, the episode's author was saying the vision was to be understood symbolically. The eating of semen, Jung suggested, may have been symbolic of Christ as the inner man who is reached by the path of self-knowledge—"the kingdom of heaven is within you."

Although Jung was "presented" with the Eid codex taken illegally out of Egypt, Page stipulated that it be returned to Cairo eventually. That was probably an inevitable arrangement because the Jung codex was only partially intact. Of five titles in what would later be termed Codex I in the Nag Hammadi library, only *The Apocryphon of James* and *The Treatise on the Resurrection* were complete. About forty missing pages were in the Dattari-Tano collection sitting in the Coptic Museum.

Agreements were reached to return the Jung codex pages to Cairo once the scholarly work was done. (The last pages were shipped to the museum in 1975.) In turn, Quispel was permitted to transcribe the rest of the Codex I pages at the museum on April 2, 1955. After watching the ropes binding the suitcase being untied, the seals broken, and small boxes of papyri opened amid "the noise of a spray can used to kill the ants," Quispel found the missing pages on top, mixed up and many of them fragmentary.

On October 5, Quispel was also granted access to *The Gospel of Thomas* in another codex. "It was a noteworthy sensation to see those words of Jesus, after fifteen centuries, loom up out of

Henri-Charles Puech, Doresse's teacher (left), and Dutch scholar Gilles Quispel (right) were at the Coptic Museum in the mid-1950s. Pahor Labib, successor to Mina as museum director, holds the magnifying glass. Photo courtesy of The Institute for Antiquity and Christianity.

obscurity, while at the back of one's thoughts one question remained: 'Are they authentic?' "

In that same year, some Gnostic writings were beginning to appear in print. The treatises discovered in 1896 were finally published in Germany by Walter Till, who was shown the Nag Hammadi versions of *The Apocryphon of John* and *The Sophia of Jesus Christ* for footnote comparisons.

Activity in Egypt picked up in 1956. Pahor Labib, director of the Coptic Museum, published page photographs from much of Codex I and parts of Codex II, including *The Gospel of Thomas* and *The Gospel of Philip*. The Egyptian government made a token payment to Tano and Miss Dattari for the confiscated manuscripts.

A ten-member international committee was appointed to publish a standardized edition of the library. Quispel and Puech, accompanied by Antoine Guillaumont of France, were the only foreigners attending a month-long organizational meeting. Elaborate plans were laid, but outside events gave a foreboding of more interruptions to come.

The two French scholars left Cairo at the end of October just as an international crisis over the use of the Suez Canal was breaking. The conflict brought French and British troops onto Egyptian soil. The Dutch scholar, Quispel, lingering until the last moment, finally left Egypt on an American ship in early November.

5. The Straits of Scholarship

From their hotel or on walks to the university, the assembled professors could squint against the April morning sunlight toward the geographical toe of Italy's boot just a few miles away. In the city of Messina, on the northeastern tip of Sicily, sixty-nine men and women from eleven countries gathered in 1966 for a conference that was the first of its kind—the International Colloquium on the Origins of Gnosticism.

The academic mix included not only scholars involved in biblical and early church studies but also those interested in the histories of religions and comparative religious studies. Such a meeting was made possible, of course, by the earthenware "time capsule" discovered in the sands of Egypt some twenty years earlier.

Responding to a broadly felt need for academic orientation in a field of study waiting to be recultivated, Ugo Bianchi and his colleagues at the University of Messina arranged the six-day colloquium in collaboration with the International Association for the History of Religions.

Even before they arrived for the April 13 opening, most participants had a good idea of what was going to be said. Organizers persuaded most of the delegates (including sixteen who could not come) to mail in advance their papers, which were mimeographed and distributed to other delegates.

Swamped with reading material, one contributor remarked, "I received five kilograms [eleven pounds] of material, but I had only time to read four kilograms." Only four papers were scheduled to be read in full, leaving time and energy for discussions and enjoyment of the Sicilian setting.

With so many professors versed in the tales of antiquity, the myths of Scylla and Charybdis kept cropping up in conversations. Scylla and Charybdis were female monsters of Greek mythology who lurked in the Straits of Messina for foolhardy navigators attempting to pass through. The once-beautiful Scylla was a six-headed ogre who would snatch men from the decks of passing ships. Charybdis used whirlpool action at the other end of the straits to suck in seawater and take along with it any passing ships. Odysseus, in his travels, narrowly escaped death at the two-mile-wide northern strait guarded by Charybdis.

When the opening paper of the colloquium was read, however, it was not Greek mythology but Iranian mythology that was the prime topic of discussion. Geo Widengren of Uppsala, Sweden, president of the International Association for the History of Religions, vigorously championed his thesis that the origins of Gnosticism could be found in the Persian religions, such as Zoroastrianism, with their tendencies to divide reality into good and evil, light and dark.

Iranian explanations met with opposition. Some suggested possible Egyptian and even Buddhist relationships. Arguments for Gnosticism's origin as a Christian heresy were presented, but generally the Christian origin theses lost out—certainly the well-known one of the nineteenth-century theologian Adolf Harnack who called Gnosticism "the acute Hellenization of Christianity." As the colloquium proceeded, increasing attention was given to Jewish influences.

Widengren hardly mentioned the Nag Hammadi discovery or its potential, but delegates were eager to hear the discussion following the second day's major paper by Martin Krause of Münster, West Germany. Between 1959 and 1961 Krause had spent considerable time cataloguing, transcribing, and photographing manuscripts in the Coptic Museum. He explained in detail at Messina what the professors already knew in general—that ten years after an international committee was formed to publish the Gnostic library (and two decades after the discovery) the Gnostics were nearly as obscure as ever!

Only thirteen of the fifty-two tractates had reached print by then, and three of those were Nag Hammadi's duplicate copies of *The Apocryphon of John.* Less than 10 percent had appeared in English translation.

The frequently inexplicable roadblocks encountered between 1956 and 1966 disturbed many. "The slow publication of the collection has thus far been shrouded in a veil of mystery—not all of it engendered by the sometimes ponderous ways of scholarship," observed George MacRae, an American Jesuit who attended the Messina meeting.

Actually, the straits of scholarship in the preceding decade had Scylla-and-Charybdis-like characteristics. The French professors, key figures on the international committee, were snatched off the scholarship deck by the 1956 Suez Canal conflict. The committee never reconvened, apparently because of the break in Egyptian-French relations. In addition, museum director Labib was miffed when his name was omitted from a 1959 publication of *The Gospel of Thomas* produced by Puech, Quispel, Guillaumont, and others, according to the Frenchmen.

In this vacuum, scholars from Scandinavia and Germany were drawn down to Cairo and came up with arbitrary assignments from Labib. Frustrating to other researchers was that "channels through which the assignments . . . have been processed are not fully clear."

UNESCO had made an agreement with Egyptian officials in 1961 to form a new international translation committee but later decided to limit itself to publishing photographs of the pages. That alone promised to be of great help: once photographs of the Nag Hammadi papyri were published, the manuscripts would be in the public domain and accessible to scholars who could read Coptic.

However, well after the U.N. agency's own deadline of March 1, 1965, only about 70 percent of the pages had been photographed. Picture taking had been anything but meticulous in arrangement of fragments, and all blank pages were not being photographed. (Sometimes a blank page would bear blottings from the opposite page. If pieces of the page with script were missing, the blottings could at times produce the missing words.)

"After some discussion (at Messina) . . ." MacRae wrote, "it was agreed that a committee should draft a report for presentation to UNESCO, urging that body to push forward its initial project by photographing the entire Nag Hammadi collection adequately and publishing photographs of all the works."

The five-hundred-word cable began: "The Nag Hammadi codices are of quite fundamental significance for the study of Gnosticism, which is of itself of considerable importance for understanding the context of ideas out of which our modern world emerged." After detailing some of the problems, the appeal ended with the "fervent wish" of the assembled scholars that the project be completed "without delay." The three-man committee that prepared the cable consisted of Martin Krause, whose speech sparked the discussion, Torgny Säve-Söderbergh of Sweden, and an American New Testament theologian, James M. Robinson.

Then forty-one, Robinson was known in some theological circles for his book *A New Quest for the Historical Jesus* and other works, but he was a relative outsider at the Messina colloquium. He felt he had been named to the committee, a position he would employ to shake loose dozens of previously inaccessible Nag Hammadi texts, for two reasons: "One, I could write a cable in English, which was the language they wanted, and two, in the discussions at the meeting, when anybody asked what was going on in Cairo—what had been photographed and the like—I had just come from Cairo and so I could say, 'Well, last week the UNESCO man there . . .' "

Robinson, a tall, lean, and intense professor from California, retained a Southern accent from his youth. He was graduating with honors from North Carolina's Davidson College and Columbia Theological Seminary about the time the Nag Hammadi manuscripts were being discovered.

Fascinated in the 1950s and early 1960s by even the limited amount of Nag Hammadi materials then available, Robinson began studying Coptic with some others while teaching at the School of Theology at Claremont (Calif.) and the Claremont Graduate School. He took a sabbatical leave in 1965–1966 at the American School of Oriental Research in Jerusalem, Jordan, "to fill in blanks in my background on the manuscript and archeological side of New Testament studies." He spent part of his time in Jerusalem "plowing through" a translation of *The Apocalypse of Adam*. Later he explored the Nag Hammadi countryside.

Just weeks before the Messina conference, Robinson visited Cairo's Coptic Museum and asked to look at the original *Apocalypse* manuscript. "They were very nice, but they told me everything was under the control of UNESCO in Paris now," Robinson said. But the UNESCO official in Cairo disclaimed any U.N.

authority over the manuscripts themselves. "In other words, I was getting the runaround," Robinson said.

Knowing that Krause had some pages photographed while he was in Cairo, Robinson went to the German Archeological Institute. The assistant director got out at least seventy sheets of photographs and, saying that he believed scholars should have access to such documents, loaned them to Robinson. "I spent three days and two nights in a dingy room in what used to be the Presbyterian mission in Cairo transcribing and proofreading the pages," recalled Robinson. "I got so that I could do about four pages an hour."

Following the Messina gathering, Robinson seized upon an offer by Krause to let the American copy his transcription of *The Letter of Peter to Philip* at Münster, West Germany. When Robinson arrived, he was informed that he was scheduled to lecture the next day. Caught unaware (a mailed request to Jerusalem missed him), Robinson was persuaded to speak by the offer to photocopy the Gnostic text transcription and allow him to prepare a lecture. Since Robinson had on hand a paper in German on Albert Schweitzer's *Quest of the Historical Jesus* that he could use for the lecture, he stayed up all night copying the rest of the notebook Krause had lent him—sixty pages from *Zostrianos*, the other Codex VIII treatise. Krause later gave Robinson page proofs to another tractate the German professor had translated and was readying for publication, *The Exegesis on the Soul.* "I was knocking myself out so I could come back to America with as many as one hundred fifty pages of otherwise inaccessible texts," Robinson said.

As early as June 1966, back in Southern California, Robinson told *Los Angeles Times* religion editor Dan L. Thrapp that he hoped to translate, study, and eventually publish some of the material. Just how he had obtained the transcriptions "he does not care to reveal," said the *Times.* Through a combination of tact, stealth, and persistence, Robinson soon would have a replica of practically the whole library.

He went to the Paris UNESCO office in 1967 in the role of secretary of the Messina ad hoc committee that had cabled the U.N. agency the year before. "I used that as an excuse to ask the man in charge there some questions," said Robinson. "Finally, he got tired of my asking him so many questions, and he said, 'You go through my file and *tell* me what I've got!' Thus, I got access to UNESCO photographs from 1967 more or less on, and in that way was able to copy out the whole library bit by bit."

Robinson organized a team of scholars, mostly Americans, for translating and analyzing the library through the newly created Institute for Antiquity and Christianity within the Claremont Graduate School, about twenty-five miles east of Los Angeles. Two other major centers for team research were formed in East Berlin, at Humboldt University under the direction of Hans-Martin Schenke, and in Quebec, at the University of Laval under Paul-Hubert Poirer.

Detailed commentaries on individual treatises began appearing in the mid-1970s, including a series for which Robinson and West Germany's Krause were co-editors. Robinson and others strove to establish models for cooperative research to replace the pattern of scholarly monopolies over selected texts—a practice that had also slowed work on the Dead Sea Scrolls for years.

The publication that guaranteed unfettered research on the Gnostic works was *The Facsimile Edition of the Nag Hammadi Codices*, eleven volumes published by E. J. Brill of Leiden, Netherlands, that appeared between 1972 and 1977. It contains the best available photographs of the pages and numerous fragments.

Negotiations for the facsimile edition, completed in the winter of 1970–1971 with UNESCO and Egypt, took Robinson on several extended visits, between teaching duties, to Paris and Cairo. Robinson also brought Doresse to Los Angeles in 1972 for the International Congress of Learned Societies in the Field of Religion, of which Robinson was a principal organizer. Doresse then presented his glossy prints of Codex I—the Eid/Jung codex—to the Claremont Institute. They proved to be helpful because some of the fragments showing in those photos had been lost during the manuscripts' intercontinental travels.

At least two-thirds of the previous manuscript photography had to be redone because of poor arrangement of the fragments or because many pages were photographed with a dark background. When a letter only partially showed on the edge of a hole (or lacuna, as it is technically called), it was difficult to tell where the dark ink left off and the dark background began. White backgrounds were used for the new photos.

Assembling the fragments was time-consuming too, but it had its rewards. The title of one treatise. *Marsanes,* was found this way.

6. The Mythical and the Historical Jesus

James M. Robinson's dedication to the Nag Hammadi Gnostic library can be explained partly by his thoroughgoing nature, but vital keys lie in his experience with European scholarship. He completed his doctorate in contemporary theology under Karl Barth of Basel, Switzerland, but while working on his dissertation he spent the winter of 1950–1951 in Marburg, West Germany. There he had a chance to hear some lectures and seminars by another theological giant of the era, Rudolf Bultmann, sixty-seven, who was to retire from teaching within months.

While teaching New Testament studies later at Emory University in Atlanta, Robinson avidly read volume after volume of Bultmann's works. "My swing from the Barthian camp into the Bultmannian took place actually after I had time to read it all," said Robinson.

A controversial figure for his "demythologizing" treatment of the New Testament, Bultmann characterized the descriptions of miraculous events, myths, and first-century worldviews presupposed by New Testament writers as natural for that period but inappropriate for twentieth-century understanding. Nevertheless, Bultmann declared that despite the ancient framework, the gospel message can still challenge modern individuals to new, liberating perspectives.

More than anything else, Bultmann's contention that Gnostic ideas were a major influence on the New Testament drove Robinson quite naturally to the Nag Hammadi studies. The discovery in Egypt offered "the golden opportunity to verify, update, revise as need be Bultmann's viewpoint on the religious context of the New Testament, which for him was primarily Gnostic," Robinson said in an interview.

Bultmann subscribed to many tenets of the "history of religions school," which tends to concentrate on the environment of a religion in its formative era and how it was shaped by history, rather than to treat any faith as supernaturally revealed unaffected by human hopes and ideas at its birth. Many Christian critics of this school object to what they see as the tendency to regard Christianity as just one religion among others.

Bultmann saw Christianity as certainly shaping its own proclamation, but also as borrowing some concepts from the religious and philosophical thought of its day, intentionally or otherwise. Judaism provided a basic body of Scripture, and the apocalyptic mood of some Jews in Jesus' day provided the idea of a messiah, resurrection of the dead, and coming divine judgment. The traditional Hellenistic culture called for a philosophical, rational approach to ideas and a Stoic detachment from the vicissitudes of life. The mystery cults spreading from Egypt, Syria, and Asia Minor also had some impact. The Christ was "conceived as a mystery deity, in whose death and Resurrection the faithful participate through the sacraments," Bultmann wrote in *Primitive Christianity in Its Contemporary Setting.*

Christianity asserts that humanity cannot redeem itself, that is, "save" itself from the world and the powers that hold sway in it. In this concept, primitive Christianity was greatly influenced by Gnostic ideas, said Bultmann. "Man's redemption," he wrote, "can only come from the divine world as an event," according to both the Gnostics and the Christians.

Most significantly, early Christians interpreted the person of Jesus to a great extent in terms of the "Gnostic redeemer myth," Bultmann contended. Jesus "is a divine figure sent down from the celestial world of light, the Son of the Most High coming forth from the Father, veiled in earthly form and inaugurating the redemption through his work." That picture of Jesus was dependent largely upon Gnostic imagery.

The Gnostic-redeemer-myth theory was not the invention of Rudolf Bultmann, but he outlined what became the classic model. Though most of the evidence he used was derived from the New Testament or later manuscripts, he considered the myth to predate Christianity's development.

As long ago as 1925, Bultmann proposed his version of the Gnostic redeemer myth and its significance for Christianity. As he summarized it years later, here are the major features of the myth, which, he added, was probably told with many variations:

The Gnostic myth tells the fate of the soul, humanity's true inner self represented as "a spark of a heavenly figure of light, the original man." In primordial times, demonic powers of darkness conquer this figure of light, tearing it into shreds.

The sparks of light are used by the demons to "create a world out of the chaos of darkness as a counterpart of the world of light, of which they were jealous." The demons closely guarded the elements of light enclosed in humans. "The demons endeavor to stupefy them and make them drunk, sending them to sleep and making them forget their heavenly home." Some people nevertheless become conscious of their heavenly origin and of the alien nature of the world. They yearn for deliverance.

"The supreme deity takes pity on the imprisoned sparks of light, and sends down the heavenly figure of light, his Son, to redeem them. This Son arrays himself in the garment of the earthly body, lest the demons should recognize him. He invites his own to join him, awakens them from their sleep, reminds them of their heavenly home, and teaches them about the way to return."

The redeemer teaches them sacred and secret passwords, for the souls will have to pass the different spheres of the planets, watchposts of the demonic cosmic powers. "After accomplishing his work, he ascends and returns to heaven again to prepare a way for his own to follow him. This they will do when they die." The redeemer's work will be completed when he is able to reassemble all the sparks of light in heaven. That done, the world will come to an end, returning to its original chaos. "The darkness is left to itself, and that is the judgment."

Bultmann, who once suggested that the author of the Gospel of John was a convert from a Gnostic sect, also thought the Fourth Gospel reflected the Gnostic redeemer myth. The oft-quoted prologue (John 1:1–18) to the Gospel is usually cited in this regard. It begins:

In the beginning was the Word, and the Word was with God, and the Word was God. He was in the beginning with God; all things were made through him, and without him was not anything made that was made.

In him was life, and the life was the light of men. The light shines in the darkness, and the darkness has not overcome it (John 1:1–5).

The wording is vague and poetic enough to have invited innumerable interpretations in the history of Christianity. Taken together with John's later narration of Jesus' ministry and significance, the prologue pictures Jesus as "the preexistent Son of God, the Word who exists with him from all eternity," says Bultmann. He is sent by God as light for the world; indeed he *is* the light, the agent of revelation.

After accomplishing his Father's mission, Jesus returns to heaven to prepare the way for his own, that they may join him. Jesus says, "I am the way, and the truth, and the life; no one comes to the Father, but by me" (John 14:6) and, "Now is the judgment of this world, now shall the ruler of this world be cast out; and I, when I am lifted up from the earth, will draw all men to myself" (John 12:31–32).

Bultmann argued that echoes of the Gnostic redeemer myth appeared in other parts of the New Testament beside the Gospel of John. Bultmann saw it, for instance, behind "a traditional hymn" used by Paul in which Christ, a preexistent being, left the celestial world to take on human form, that of a servant (Phil. 2:6–11).

By attempting to separate out the mythical images attached to Jesus by the first generations of believers, Bultmann inadvertently encouraged students who hoped to step closer to the historical Jesus. Bultmann himself suggested it was not possible to reach the Jesus of history, but his learned opinions on why certain sayings of Jesus should or should not be considered authentic are still consulted today in that quest.

What Bultmann could not have anticipated was the appearance of an ancient sayings collection. *The Gospel of Thomas* was an unexpected resource for specialists who sought an improved picture of Jesus through his individual sayings—rather than via "biographical" but theologically creative Gospels. Regardless of the Gnostic tone of many sayings, *Thomas* demonstrated that some early believers revered Jesus primarily as a teacher of wisdom; in the New Testament Gospels that is only one of his aspects. Upon the first descriptions of the format of *Thomas*, New

Testament scholars also knew that the theory was strengthened for the onetime existence of Q, a sayings collection thought to have been used by the Gospels of Matthew and Luke. A copy of Q has never been found, but many New Testament scholars have been convinced that it was a meaningful work in itself, despite the absence of a narrative on Jesus' life and death.

Robinson was one of the earliest New Testament scholars to argue for *Thomas*'s value in this regard. An article of his, first published in 1964, traced how "the words of the wise" was an honored tradition in the early church, sometimes taking on the nature of riddlelike, or "secret," sayings such as the sayings in Mark 4. In that article, later incorporated into a book of coauthored with Helmut Koester, *Trajectories Through Early Christianity*, Robinson said he was following the suggestions of Bultmann about the affinity between Jewish wisdom sayings and the sayings of Jesus, a literary genre best represented in Bultmann's day in the postulated Q document. Indeed, once he considered the Claremont Institute's Nag Hammadi project essentially completed in 1984, Robinson launched into a project with other scholars to reconstruct Q from its representations in Matthew and Luke.

Thus, Robinson's attraction to the Nag Hammadi library was fueled by the prospect of settling two questions raised by Bultmann: were some gnostic myths forerunners of the Christian image of Jesus as a heavenly redeemer? Could a clearer relationship be established between the wisdom movement in Judaism and the early wisdom teaching of Jesus?

The American scholar's office has one wall serving as a photographic gallery of noted theologians. Not surprisingly, occupying the honored spot in the center is a picture of Rudolf Bultmann.

7. Return to the Cliffs

Although Robinson was drawn to the Nag Hammadi library by the chance to prove, disprove, or improve Rudolf Bultmann's theories about primitive Christianity, the American professor did relatively little writing about the contents in the first decade after the pivotal Messina colloquium. Robinson's attention to the archeological side took much of his time, starting with the effort to photograph and catalog each page and piece of papyrus.

He was also unsatisfied with the hazy information about the manuscript discovery. Robinson had obtained a few leads when he visited the Nag Hammadi area twice in the spring of 1966. However, he had to wait seven years to follow them up: the Egyptian countryside was closed to foreigners from the Six-Day War in June 1967 until November 1, 1974. He returned to Nag Hammadi toward the end of November 1974 and again in January 1975. Then, in the last half of 1975, he picked up a trail that had been cold for a quarter of a century.

Robinson had learned that the Coptic Museum's purchase of Codex III, which Mina had shown to Jean Doresse in September 1947, was recorded in the museum's registry of acquisitions. The entry, written in Arabic, said that the seventy leaves of papyrus manuscript were bought for 250 pounds from Raghib Andarawus and received October 4, 1946. This was "the decisive clue to the reconstruction of the story" of the discovery, Robinson said.

"I asked Abram Bibawi, then sub-principal of the Boys' Secondary School of Nag Hammadi, if he had heard that name. He replied that he had studied under him!" Robinson said.

Robinson was introduced by Bibawi to a man who lived across the Nile at Al-Qasr, known as Chenoboskia in the Greco-Roman period. That villager directed Robinson to Raghib Andarawus, who was his uncle. But, more than that, the villager introduced Robinson to his neighbor in Al-Qasr, Muhammad Ali. This man,

Muhammad Ali, the discoverer of the manuscripts, in Al-Qasr (ancient Chenoboskia) with a Coptic monastery in the background. Photo courtesy of The Institute for Antiquity and Christianity.

then fifty-six years old when Robinson first interviewed him on September 16, 1975, was the principal discoverer of the manuscripts!

From Ali and other members of his family, Robinson was able to construct the following account:

Not long before the Coptic church Christmas of January 7, 1946—evidently in December 1945—Muhammad Ali, two of his brothers, and four other camel drivers were digging for *sabakh* midway up the sloping base of Jabal al-Tarif not far from the hamlet of Hamrah Dum. December is the usual month when the natives of the region dig for the soft soil to fertilize the hard ground of the grain fields. Muhammad's brother Abu al-Majd, then fifteen, unearthed a large reddish jar. It was about 60 centimeters in height and had four small handles near the top. The opening had been covered with a bowl and apparently sealed with bitumen. (A third brother, Khalifah Ali, later took the bowl to someone who kept it through the years. Robinson, who eventually acquired it, said a few black tarlike stains can be seen on the bowl.)

With the discovery of the sealed jar, Muhammad Ali, at twenty-six the oldest brother, took charge. He at first feared to break it open, thinking that inside there might be a jinn, an evil spirit. "But on reflecting that it might contain treasure, he regained his courage," Robinson said. Ali raised his mattock and smashed the jar.

"Out swirled golden-like particles that disappeared into the sky—neither jinns nor gold but perhaps papyrus fragments!" Robinson said. Muhammad decided to divide the books among all seven in the digging party. Since there were not enough to give each person two codices, he gave each man one complete codex and tore out parts of the others to make the division even. The other camel drivers, for some reason, renounced their claims to the manuscripts. Muhammad "then stacked the lots back together in a pile, unwound his white headdress, knotted them in it, and slung the whole bundle over his shoulder," Robinson said.

After riding his camel back home to Al-Qasr, he dumped the books, loose leaves, and fragments on the ground. Unfortunately, they lay near some straw by a large oven used for baking bread. Muhammad's mother, Umm Ahmad, conceded to Robinson that "she burned much of the ripped-out papyrus and broken covers . . . in the oven along with the straw."

Thus, the rumor Doresse had heard—that natives used some papyrus leaves for heating their tea—was not far off. Robinson has concluded that the library's missing leaves—the great majority of Codex XII and probably of Codex X, plus some individual leaves in other codices, most notably nine from Codex III—were probably lost in this period right after the discovery.

Part of Robinson's concern to track down the circumstances of the discovery was to make sure that all that could be found was indeed already found. After all, the discovery of the Dead Sea Scrolls was really a series of discoveries in caves overlooking the Dead Sea region. Jabal al-Tarif is honeycombed with over a hundred and fifty caves—some natural niches and others openings just large enough to receive a sarcophagus. Doresse had alluded to the possibility of a sepulchre or tomb as the discovery site.

But Robinson found that getting Muhammad Ali to point out the spot himself was extremely difficult. Incredibly, Muhammad Ali said he had not been back to the discovery site in thirty years—despite the fact that it was only six kilometers away from his village! Ali's fear, Robinson soon learned, arose from a vicious blood feud, one that went back to May 1945.

It was then that Muhammad Ali's father, while guarding irrigation machinery in fields near Al-Qasr, killed and beheaded a person taken to be a thief. The alleged thief was from Hamrah Dum, the hamlet close to the cliff. The next day, Muhammad Ali found his father shot through the head and the body lying next to the head of his father's victim.

All was quiet in December 1945 when Muhammad Ali and six others discovered the papyrus-filled jar. But about a month later, Ali's family saw an opportunity for revenge. Muhammad Ali was told that the murderer of his father was lying asleep in the heat of the day by the road in Al-Qasr. A jar of molasses he had for sale sat beside him. The purported murderer was Ahmad Ismail, son of the sheriff who had been imposed on Al-Qasr by the fierce Hawara tribe living at Hamrah Dum. Upon learning this, Muhammad Ali's mother, "who had told her seven sons to keep their mattocks sharp, handed these instruments to her sons to avenge her," Robinson wrote. "They fell upon Ahmad Ismail pitilessly. Abu al-Majd, then a teenager, brags that he struck the first blow straight to the head. After having hacked Ahmad Ismail to pieces limb by limb, they cut out his heart and consumed it among them—the ultimate act of blood revenge." For the lack of cooperative witnesses, the crime officially went unsolved.

The Al-Samman clan, to which Muhammad Ali's family belonged, was numerous enough in Al-Qasr to feel relatively secure when they stayed close to town. Nevertheless, about three months after Ahmad Ismail was slain, the victim's brother managed to kill two from the Al-Samman clan. It didn't end at that, however. Eleven years later, in 1957, a son of Ahmad Ismail, twenty-two years old, went with a friend to the edge of Al-Qasr where the Muhammad Ali family was taking part in a funeral procession. They killed about ten people with gunfire from automatic weapons. Nearly twenty years after the assault, in 1975, Muhammad Ali proudly showed Robinson the scar from a wound above his heart and swore that if he ever caught the son of Ahmad Ismail, he would kill him.

Despite that boast, Muhammad Ali flatly refused to return to

James M. Robinson, the
New Testament scholar
from Claremont, California,
tracked down the discoverer
of the manuscripts. Here he
sits outside a cave in the
side of Jabal al-Tarif. Photo
courtesy of The Institute
for Antiquity and
Christianity.

the cliffs until the American offered him some money. Even
then, however, Ali agreed only with certain conditions: Ali would
be dressed in American clothes and sit with Robinson in the back
of a Russian-made jeep owned by the director of the Nag Hammadi sugar factory. The jeep's owner, Hanny M. al-Zeiny, was
to sit in front. The day they went was September 17, 1975, during the Islamic month of Ramadan, an annual period of daytime
fasting. Ali purposely suggested going to the cliff late in the
afternoon when hunger and thirst would have kept most local
residents indoors.

Unfortunately, when the party drove by the cliffs Ali pointed
toward one of the caves as the discovery site. After a careful
search of the tomb, it was decided that this could not have been
the place where a large jar once was buried.

A few weeks later, Muhammad Ali was confronted and challenged to try again. On December 11, 1975, he went by car to
the area and walked straight toward a broken boulder about
halfway up the slope of the cliff. He pointed to a spot that in

fact Jean Doresse had photographed in 1950 as the area of the find.

Robinson and his associates found no additional evidence that this was the jar's hiding place, but he later concluded that the talus, or rock-strewn slope at the base of the cliff, was a reasonable location as the burial spot. The nearest cave to the discovery site was one that Jean and Marianne Doresse had described, the one with the opening verses of psalms painted in red on the walls, indicating that Coptic Christian monks may have used the cave for a place of meditation. Who placed the manuscripts into the jar sometime in the late fourth century remains unknown. It seems unlikely that it was one collection from one of the nearby Coptic monasteries. Robinson observed that the duplicate texts made it more likely that they were several private collections. *The Apocryphon of John* was a favorite, appearing in the front of three different codices. Two copies each were also found of *The Gospel of the Egyptians*, *The Gospel of Truth*, and an untitled text later named *On the Origin of the World*.

In addition to locating the discoverer, Robinson was able to trace the routes the manuscripts took out of the Nag Hammadi area. Muhammad Ali's family received little more than sugar, tea, oranges, or small cash amounts for the books, but others in the area with business contacts were more fortunate. A gold merchant in Nag Hammadi and a grain merchant in the region sold some manuscripts in Cairo. But most of the books were obtained by Bahij Ali, a man Robinson described as "the one-eyed outlaw of Al-Qasr." Accompanied by an antiquities dealer, Bahij Ali sold his whole stock to Phocion J. Tano, the antiquities dealer in Cairo. Tano obtained some more leaves by going to Nag Hammadi and may have paid just under 2,000 pounds for his lot. Tano told Robinson that he received British and Swiss offers of 100,000 pounds for them, but that after the manuscripts were placed under government control he received only 5,000 pounds.

Codex III, the first acquisition of the Coptic Museum, made its way to Cairo by a different route. In early 1946, after the slaying of Ahmad Ismail, Muhammad Ali's home was often being searched for weapons by police. Apparently not wanting to provide any pretext for his arrest, Ali left the books at the home of a Coptic priest. The priest's brother-in-law, Raghib Andarawus, mentioned earlier, saw Codex III and persuaded the priest to give it to him. Andarawus took it to Cairo but had a series of disappointments. Andarawus eventually sold the codex to the Coptic Museum under pressure from the government Department of Antiquities, which learned of the book.

That codex was the first one seen by Jean Doresse, but, Robinson learned, Doresse was not the first Westerner to cast discerning eyes on samples of the Nag Hammadi find. Museum Director Togo Mina had shown Codex III to two Europeans on December 5, 1946. One of them, Francois Daumas, then discussed what he had seen with French scholar Antoine Guillaumont the next summer in Paris. Daumas returned to Cairo in November 1947, but Mina had already made publishing plans with Doresse.

Also in 1946, Father B. Couroyer, a Coptologist in Jerusalem, was sent photographs of four pages from Codex I. Albert Eid, who was hoping to sell Codex I to the University of Michigan, sent Couroyer's brief report to the university library in a letter dated January 13, 1947.

Couroyer identified the Coptic dialect used and, from only two pages of *The Apocryphon of James*, correctly characterized the writing as "a dialogue of our Lord with his disciples, especially with St. James." The priest-scholar compared it to the postresurrection dialogue seen in *Pistis Sophia*, then one of the few known Gnostic Christian works. But Couroyer said this composition was distinctive. "One finds oneself on the border between orthodox theology and Gnosticism," Couroyer wrote. "In the case of the present manuscript I do not believe that one is in the presence of a purely Gnostic work."

Within a year of its discovery, Robinson observed, one important Nag Hammadi writing "was provided with a remarkably accurate analysis." It would be the first of many scholarly surprises once the entrepreneurial intrigue and academic rivalries ran their course. Even as Robinson was uncovering the full story of the manuscript discovery, studies of the contents were prompting startling conclusions about the origins of the Gnostic movement.

II. THE JEWISH CONNECTION

8. Dangerous Speculations

Early rabbis considered parts of the Bible too dangerous to discuss publicly or without mature guidance. Johanan ben Zakkai, a Jewish teacher prominent in the years after 70 C.E., passed along a series of warnings: the laws concerning incest should not be taught before more than two people; the Genesis story of creation should not be taught before more than one; the fantastic visions of God's throne-chariot in the book of Ezekiel should not be taught before even one—unless that one is a knowledgeable sage himself; and it's better never to have lived than to speculate over what is above, below, beyond, and in the opposite beyond. "And whosoever has no regard for the honor of his Creator," concluded Zakkai, "it were better for him had he not come into the world."

Could Johanan ben Zakkai have been thinking about the Gnostics with this advice? Gnostic heretics are not mentioned specifically in Jewish rabbinic literature, but some modern studies have shown "there were heretical Jewish Gnostics in Palestine, and they were referred to as *minim*," according to Birger Pearson of the University of California at Santa Barbara. In some cases, the *minim* may have been Jewish Christians, but Pearson maintains that the polemic in rabbinic writings makes it clear that Jewish Gnostics, from the early second century on, if not earlier, "posed a great threat in many Jewish circles."

A certain amount of mysticism was tolerated by the Jewish sages in those days. The late Gershom Scholem, an authority on Jewish mysticism, contended that some precursors of the elaborate Kabbalah speculations of medieval European Jews can be traced as far back as the first century B.C.E. in Palestine. Early Jewish mystics focused on the first chapters of Genesis and the opening chapter of Ezekiel. In the latter, the prophet Ezekiel describes his heavenly visions. God was borne on a shining chariot the four wheels of which were accompanied by four-faced living creatures. Amid great brilliance, the Lord himself appeared to Ezekiel like a human form—half gleaming bronze, half fire—seated on a sapphirelike throne.

Zakkai's warning against teaching about Ezekiel's visions may have been directed to mystically inclined Jews. Although Scholem referred to Jewish "gnostics" in this period, these were people still faithful to the biblical God.

Worse than throne mysticism, in Zakkai's mind, was that someone would have "no regard for the honor of the Creator"—and the seething sarcasm in certain Nag Hammadi texts fits that description. Though it has been difficult to conceive of Jews who would hold such attitudes and could still be Jewish by definition, studies have shown that the first centuries B.C.E. and C.E. represented a religiously unsettled period.

Judaism then was hardly the uniform religion described by later rabbis. "Prior to 70 A.D., there was no recognized 'orthodoxy,'" writes David Syme Russell. "Nor was there any one party whose beliefs formed the norm by which Judaism could be judged."

About 63 B.C.E. when the Roman Empire first exercised power over the Israelites, the authority to interpret Jewish law passed from the priestly aristocracy known as the Sadducees to the more liberal and popular Pharisees. The Sadducees preferred to keep the sacrificial cult activities centered at the Jerusalem Temple rather than allow ritual purity laws to be practiced in Jewish homes, as advocated by the Pharisees. The Roman destruction of the Jerusalem Temple in 70 C.E. eliminated the Sadducees' chief function.

The Pharisees apparently became more widely referred to as "rabbis" after 70 C.E. Yet it has been said that no one imagines that the day after the Temple's destruction someone like Johanan ben Zakkai woke up and said, "Today I am a rabbi." Historian Jacob Neusner has suggested that the rabbinic tradition developed from the piety of the Pharisaic sect and the professional ideals of the scribes.

Two other religious groups of that period were the Essenes and the Zealots. Seeking righteousness, many Essenes led severely restricted lives. They believed in the immortality of the soul and were nonconformist about Temple rituals. They were also thought to be pacifist, although the Qumran community of that sect as revealed by the Dead Sea Scrolls nurtured some military aspirations. The Zealots were known mainly for their unsuccessful revolt against the Romans in 6 C.E., involvement in the wider revolt of 66–70, and their last-ditch stand at Masada, which fell in 73.

Much of that picture of Jewish religious movements was provided by Josephus, a Jewish commander turned Roman historian. In his longest work, *Jewish Antiquities*, completed in 93 C.E., Josephus also mentions the executions of John the Baptist, Jesus, and Jesus' brother, James.

John the Baptist was believed to have headed only one of a number of Jewish baptist sects. And, of course, Jesus was the inspiration for a religious movement that eventually became so unlike Judaism that it could no longer be classified as a Jewish sect.

Religious literature in this period also illustrates the diversity of spiritual expression. Apocalyptic essays predicted cataclysmic events in which evil forces would be destroyed. It was "essentially a literature of the oppressed who saw no hope for the nation simply in terms of politics or on the plane of human history," Russell writes.

The books that make up the Jewish Scriptures were already completed; the last was Daniel, which was probably written about 165 B.C.E. Daniel has been called the first and greatest of the Jewish apocalyptic writings. It may have been prompted by the anti-Jewish religious measures of the hellenized Syrian ruler Antiochus IV Epiphanes. Two later apocalyptic books in general circulation—*Jubilees* and *1 Enoch*—were held in honor by the Qumran Essenes, who also produced apocalyptic literature of their own. Both the newly found Qumran texts and previously known Jewish apocalyptic works expressed faith in the God of Israel. At the same time, their inclusion of demons, angels, last-day prophecies, astrology, and cosmology showed the impact that the eclectic, religiously concerned Hellenistic age was having on Jewish religion.

Hope for a miraculous intervention by God permeated the typical apocalyptic book. "The expression of this belief is at times fanciful and exaggerated; but book after book throbs with the passionate conviction that all God had promised would surely come to pass," Russell says.

One might guess that unfulfilled hopes could turn into bitter rejection by some believers. One scholar held for years that the destruction of the Jerusalem Temple in 70 C.E. might have given birth to the Gnostic movement. But others studying the Gnostic phenomenon have doubted that shattered Jewish apocalyptic hopes would have been transformed into the intellectualized otherworldly speculations of the Gnostics.

Apocalyptic thinking, however, might have contributed to the Gnostic viewpoint. The distance between the ordinary world and the heavenly glory was heightened in apocalyptic writing. Angels and other intermediaries materialized to bridge the gap between God and humans. God's mysteries and knowledge of the future are revealed only to "the elect" through the human visionaries described in such books.

Beside apocalyptic writings, another important literary trend in Jewish antiquity was the wisdom, or "sapiential," tradition. The early Jewish wisdom literature may be dated between the fourth and first centuries B.C.E. Old Testament examples are Proverbs, Job, and Ecclesiastes. In the Apocrypha, found in some Bibles, the genre is well represented by the Wisdom of Solomon and Ecclesiasticus, also called Sirach. The figure of Wisdom, so important when reinterpreted in Gnostic works, was often central to the Jewish sapiential writing.

"Wisdom is a figure closely connected with God, and even representing him, whether at the creation, or in the guidance of Israel, or the guidance of pious individuals; the whole history of salvation is under her control," writes Kurt Rudolph. "She protects her own and helps them to the knowledge of God; she is like a redeemer who grants immortality." Lady Wisdom eventually becomes identified in Jewish literature with religious law, the Torah, and stays with Israel.

But a pessimism ran through some of the wisdom literature and it even shows up in *1 Enoch*, basically an apocalyptic book. "Wisdom went forth to make her dwelling among the children of men, and found no dwelling place: Wisdom returned to her place and took her seat among the angels. And unrighteousness went forth from her chambers" (*1 Enoch* 42:2–3).

The apocalyptic and wisdom traditions were not opposites; they sometimes intermingled in Jewish thought in the pre-Christian era. One difference existed, however. The apocalyptic writer could reach the heavenly mysteries through intermediaries or draw upon tales of heavenly journeys by Ezra, Enoch, or Baruch, but in the wisdom genre God tended to be more inscrutable for humans.

"He is removed into the distance and placed high above earthly concerns so that his acts in history and his acts of creation become veiled," writes Rudolph, citing Job 28 and Proverbs 30:1–4. In Ecclesiastes, written about 200 B.C.E., Rudolph says, the pious person finds it difficult to discover sense and purpose in the world. "He feels himself alone and abandoned in a chaotic world in which there is no longer a fixed order of life. Despair and skepticism spread. . . . The future is uncertain, death alone is certain. Chance and fate rule the world," according to Rudolph. "The pious [person] still believes in God and his righteous guidance in the last resort; but it is rather an act of despair and a flight from perplexity."

Thus, both apocalyptic and wisdom works spoke of a remote God separated from the chaotic world. "It seems to me that the gnostic world view could take root and flower in this soil," concludes Rudolph in his 1977 book *Gnosis*. Rudolph observes that the higher "unknown God" and the despicable Creator God in Gnostic revisionism share the traits of the Jewish God of conventional sacred writings. Gnosticism, he says, was born of "a critical self-dissolution on the fringes of Judaism."

Rudolph's book, a sweeping analysis that takes into account the Nag Hammadi studies, was written while he was a history of religions professor at Karl Marx University in Leipzig, East Germany. An English translation of the book was published in 1983 while he was teaching in the United States. He, in effect, defected, then taught for two years at the University of California at Santa Barbara. In 1986, Rudolph accepted a prestigious professorship in the history of religions at the University of Marburg in West Germany.

Rudolph's conclusions are an example of what many feel is a consensus on the Jewish origin of Gnostic religious thought. Among the first scholars to propose Jewish origins was Gilles

Quispel of the Netherlands, who was involved in acquiring the so-called Jung codex. As Quispel puts it, the characteristic features of Gnostic religion "originated in Palestine among rebellious and heterodox Judaism," and Gnosticism proper was born "at the fringe of Judaism."

The initial resistance to that theory was best stated by philosopher Hans Jonas, who argued that more evidence was necessary to assert that Jews turned against their own God so vehemently. Jonas authored a classic book on Gnosticism, *The Gnostic Religion*, based primarily on pre–Nag Hammadi resources, however. Disagreeing with some of Quispel's theses, Jonas said he would favor the origin of Gnosticism geographically close to the Jews with enough exposure for Judaism to act as a catalyst—but not with a starting point within Judaism. The Gnostic spirit, particularly as seen in *The Apocryphon of John*, Jonas said, is one "of vilification, of parody and caricature, of conscious perversion of meaning, wholesale reversal of value signs, savage degrading of the sacred—of gleefully shocking blasphemy."

That kind of mockery indeed exists in some of the books found near Nag Hammadi, as we shall soon see. Nevertheless, the Jewish elements emerged as the primary sources within *The Apocryphon of John, The Apocalypse of Adam, The Nature (Hypostasis) of the Archons, The Testimony of Truth*, and other works—even though most of the writings underwent later revisions by Christianized Gnostics. Researchers proposing Jewish beginnings, as might be expected, varied slightly in what they saw as the propelling forces.

It must be conceived as an internal revolt against Judaism, maintained George MacRae in the early 1970s when he was executive secretary of the Society of Biblical Literature. The Jesuit priest was acting dean of the Harvard Divinity School when he died in 1985. "The familiarity which Gnostic sources show toward details of Jewish thought is hardly one we could expect non-Jews to have," he said.

The key to the Gnostic attitude is that the wisdom of the God of Israel was considered by Gnostics to be a disillusionment, even a deception, MacRae suggested. Room still exists in the theory for a foreign influence, for without it the Jewish loss of confidence is unexplainable, he said. "Whether of Orphic or Neo-

Platonist or Iranian or other origin," MacRae said, "it . . . intrudes upon a form of Jewish thought and expression to drive it toward what we know as Gnosticism," he said.

Birger Pearson, a leading American proponent of the theory of a Jewish origin, agrees with those who say that peculiar brands of Christian and pagan Gnosticism developed on their own. Yet "the earliest Gnostic literature was produced by Jewish intellectuals, as a product of their revolt against the Jewish God in his capacity as World-Creator and Lawgiver." These were "religious intellectuals," not secularized unbelievers, Pearson said at a major 1983 seminar on Gnosticism.

From certain Nag Hammadi writings, Pearson said, "we can see how specifically *Jewish* literature (especially the Bible), *Jewish* exegetical and theological traditions, and *Jewish* literary genres have been utilized to express a drastic reorientation of values and perceived religious truth."

9. The Envious God and the Wise Serpent

As odd as it sounds, scholars working with ancient manuscripts often take delight in studying a clumsily written composition. If a work is lucid, it means the writer blended original ideas with older sources into a coherent piece, sometimes making it hard to estimate its age and provenance. On the other hand, writings containing sections that are distinctly different in wording and thought tend to expose the document's sources. If the transitions are abrupt, the task is easier.

Just such a source—in this case, an early Jewish Gnostic commentary on Genesis—was found "buried" within the Nag Hammadi treatise *The Testimony of Truth*, which is otherwise Christian Gnostic in content.

Following a passage contrasting the virgin birth of Jesus with the natural birth of John the Baptist and an exhortation to seek after "mysteries," a horizontal line appears in the left-hand margin of the papyrus page. The scribe was indicating a break in the account, but as Birger Pearson explains: "A source critic would see at this point—even without the scribe's mark—a clearly defined 'seam.' . . . We are encountering a literary source, previously existing and well-defined."

Inserted into *The Testimony of Truth* at this point was a primitive Gnostic midrash, or commentary, on the first couple's eating of the forbidden fruit (Gen. 3) plus some caustic observations about the Creator.

It is written in the Law concerning this, when God gave a command to Adam, "From every [tree] you may eat, [but] from the tree which is the midst of Paradise do not eat, for on the day that you eat from it you will surely die."

But the serpent was wiser than all the animals that were in Paradise, and he persuaded Eve, saying, "On the day when you eat from the tree which is in the midst of Paradise the eyes of your mind will be opened."

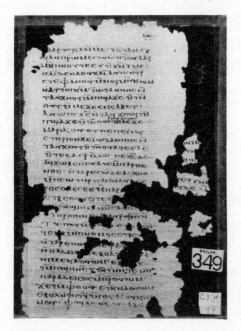

A page from *The Testimony of Truth* reveals a scribe's line in the left margin that indicates an abrupt transition in the text to an earlier, Jewish source. Photo courtesy of The Institute for Antiquity and Christianity.

And Eve obeyed, and she stretched forth her hand; she took from the tree and ate; she also gave to her husband with her. And immediately they knew that they were naked, and they took some fig leaves (and) put them on as girdles.

But [God] came at the time of [evening] walking in the midst [of] Paradise. When Adam saw him he hid himself.

And he said, "Adam, where are you?"

He answered (and) said, "[I] have come under the fig tree."

And at that very moment God [knew] that he had eaten from the tree of which he had commanded him, "Do not eat of it." And he said to him, "Who is it who has instructed you?" And Adam answered, "The woman whom you have given me."

And the woman said, "The serpent is the one who instructed me."

And he (God) cursed the serpent, and he called him "devil." And he said, "Behold, Adam has become like one of us, knowing evil and good." Then he said, "Let us cast him out of Paradise lest he take from the tree of life and eat and live for ever."

But of what sort is this God?

First [he] maliciously refused Adam from eating of the tree of knowledge. And secondly he said, "Adam, where are you?" And God does not have foreknowledge; (otherwise), would he not know from the beginning?

[And] afterwards he said, "Let us cast him [out] of this place, lest he eat of the tree of life and live for ever." Surely he has shown himself to be a malicious grudger.

And what kind of a God is this? For great is the blindness of those who read, and they did not know him. And he said, "I am the jealous God; I will bring the sins of the fathers upon the children until three (and) four generations" [see Exod. 20:5].

And he said, "I will make their heart thick, and I will cause their mind to become blind, that they might not know or comprehend the things that are said" [see Isa. 6:10].

But these things he has said to those who believe in him [and] serve him!

The next passages mention other snakes in Scripture, including the episode in Exodus 7:8–12 of Moses' rod transforming into a snake before the pharaoh. Then, *The Testimony of Truth* identifies the bronze serpent in Numbers 21:9 with Christ—indicating that the Christian writer has moved beyond the borrowed material. (The biblical citations here and above are not actually present in *The Testimony of Truth* but rather are provided for the reader's convenience.)

The commentary on Genesis 3 is anti-Jewish in any ordinary understanding of what it means to be Jewish. Yet, Pearson says, it "is replete with specifically Jewish traditions of biblical interpretation, such as could hardly have been available to people not thoroughly acquainted with jewish aggadah." The Aggadah, or Haggadah, amounted to the "retelling" of the historical and religious (but not the legal) passages of Jewish Scripture.

But for a "Gnostic," obviously, the withholding of knowledge by the Creator God was an awful judgment. By casting the first couple out of Paradise, the ancient commentator wrote, "surely he has shown himself to be a malicious grudger." In retelling the Adam and Eve story, the Jewish Gnostic writer asks sarcastically, "what kind of God is this?" and rails at the "blindness" of Jewish believers who could not see this in other biblical passages as well.

Pearson notes that the snake was described as "wiser" than any other wild creature—not "more subtle," as in Genesis 3:1. However, "wise" was an adjective consistent with Jewish commentary of the time: one early rabbinic source said the snake was "wise for evil." A saying attributed to one Rabbi Meir asserts that "the wisdom of the serpent was so great" that God had to inflict a penalty "proportionate to his wisdom"—he was cursed and condemned to crawl forever.

The comments in the source used in *The Testimony of Truth* brashly characterized the Hebrew God as arrogant, ignorant, and envious. Yet God was still referred to as *God*. However, God does acquire derogatory names in two other Gnostic works, *The Hypostasis of the Archons* and *The Apocryphon of John*. The serpent and Eve became heroic figures in *The Hypostasis of the Archons* (translated "The Reality, or Nature, of the Rulers") and in a later writing, *On the Origin of the World*.

The latter book, *Origin*, is not as important as the other two for demonstrating "the Jewish connection," but it testifies further to the bewildering variations in retelling the Genesis story. Details vary in each copy of *The Apocryphon of John*, for instance.

The word *archon* needs explaining. A term used commonly by Gnostics for the Hebrew God, it literally means "ruler" in Greek, the *lingua franca* of the Hellenistic age in eastern Mediterranean lands. The Creator was sometimes called the "First Archon" or the "Great Archon" to distinguish him from his malicious associates, also called "archons," "powers," or "authorities."

Why is the Creator God depicted as merely the head of a collective force? Gnostic Jews, looking at Scripture for the story behind the story, could hardly miss the use of the first-person plural—"Let us make man in our image, after our likeness" (Gen. 1:26) and "Behold, the man has become like one of us, knowing good and evil" (Gen. 3:22). The expulsion of humanity's forebears from Paradise, in the Gnostic view, was by an evil cabal, the "archenemies," if you will.

Finally, the version of *The Hypostasis of the Archons* found at Nag Hammadi is acknowledged to have undergone additions from an editor influenced by Christian writings. The text cites words of "the great apostle" (Paul) on "the authorities of the darkness" (Col. 1:13) that "our contest is not against flesh and [blood]; rather, the authorities of the universe and the spirits of wickedness" (Eph. 6:12). Christian influences have also been seen in the ending of *Archons*. Elaine Pagels of Princeton cites several more examples of how *Archons* seems to draw on Pauline terminology and themes, thereby proposing that the work was written in a Christian milieu. But Pearson and others seem convinced that the great bulk of *Archons* was composed in a non-Christian, Jewish-oriented context.

A synopsis of the story in *Archons*, with some references to related passages in *Apocryphon* and *Origin*, should illustrate how Jewish Scripture was reworked radically and combined with speculation about what is above, below, and beyond. In what may have been the original beginning of *Archons*, the author said the chief of the cosmic powers "is blind." Because of his power, ignorance, and arrogance, he declared he was God and that there was no one beside him, a passage echoing Isaiah 46:9.

When he so boasts, the chief archon is reproached from above. Once he is called "Samael," the "god of the blind," and another time "Sakla." The author wrote that the alternate name for Sakla is "Ialdabaoth." These three epithets for God occur in other Nag Hammadi texts with variations in spelling. The longer versions of *The Apocryphon of John* say simply and with derision, "The archon who is weak has three names. The first is Yaltabaoth, the second is Saklas, and the third is Samael. And he is impious in his arrogance which is in him."

The insults are apparently all derived from Aramaic, a Semitic language similar to Hebrew and spoken in Palestine and Syria. Sakla means "fool" in Aramaic and was a name for Satan in Judaism. Samael means the "blind god" in Aramaic; in Jewish lore it was often the angel of death. The derivation of Ialdabaoth is less sure. One suggestion is that it combines two Aramaic words meaning "begetter of" and "Sabaoth." Sabaoth in Jewish Scripture is the aspect of God that heads the heavenly armies.

The myth in *Archons* starts in the highest realms.

Within limitless eternal realms (aeons) dwells incorruptibility. Wisdom (Sophia), who is called faith (Pistis), wanted to create something, alone without her consort; and her product was a celestial thing.

A veil exists between the world above and the realms (aeons) that are below; and shadow came into being beneath the veil; and that shadow became matter; and that shadow was projected apart. And what she created became a product in the matter, like an aborted fetus. And it assumed a plastic form molded out of shadow, and became an arrogant beast resembling a lion. . . .

Opening his eyes he saw a vast quantity of matter without limit; and he became arrogant, saying, "It is I who am God, and there is none apart from me."

When he said this, he sinned against the entirety. And a voice came forth from above the realm of absolute power, saying, "You are mistaken, Samael"—which is "god of the blind."

And he said, "If any other thing exists before me, let it become visible to me!" And immediately wisdom (Sophia) stretched forth her finger and introduced light into matter; and she pursued it down to the region of chaos. And she returned up [to] her light. . . .

This ruler (archon), by being androgynous, made itself a vast realm, an extent without limit. And he contemplated creating offspring for himself, and created for himself seven offspring, androgynous just like their parent.

And he said to his offspring, "It is I who am the god of the entirety." And life (Zoe), the daughter of faith wisdom (Pistis Sophia), cried out and said to it, "You are mistaken, Sakla!"—for the alternate name is Yaltabaoth. She breathed into his face, and her breath became a fiery angel for her; and that angel bound Yaltabaoth and cast him down into Tartaros below the abyss.

Archons then relates a unique story of Sabaoth, an offspring of the chief archon, switching allegiance and singing praises to wisdom (Sophia) and her daughter, life (Zoe). In return, the feminine powers placed him in charge of the seventh heaven, just below the veil concealing the highest heavens. A rare piece of throne-chariot speculation shows up here: Sabaoth "made himself a huge four-faced chariot of cherubim, and infinitely many angels to act as ministers, and also harps and lyres."

Meanwhile, the archons had seen the image of God/incorruptibility reflected in the watery regions of Creation. They tried to grasp it but couldn't. It prompted them to create a human being in hopes of capturing the essence of incorruptibility. They used dirt to build Adam's body, modeled after both their own bodies and the celestial image they saw. The chief archon breathed into Adam's face. Adam became animate, but he could not stand up—despite days of mighty blowing by the frustrated rulers.

Declaring that all these events happened according to the will of the highest God, "the Father of the entirety," the author

writes that the Spirit came forth from a celestial level where a
heavenly prototype of Adam had existed. The Spirit entered into
the earthly Adam. Still unable to rise up from the ground, Adam
named all the beasts and birds of the earth rounded up by the
rulers. Then the archons moved Adam to the Garden to main-
tain it—but with the warning not to eat of the tree that granted
one the ability to recognize good and evil.

The scheming archons made Adam fall into a deep sleep (see
Gen. 2:21). They opened up Adam's side, removing from him
the spiritual element, and patched up Adam's side with flesh in
place of his female/spiritual part. Thus, the author writes, Adam
was endowed only with soul, or animate material.

What happened to Adam's rib? *Archons* makes no mention of
it. *The Apocryphon of John* bluntly dismisses the notion—"And not
as Moses said, 'his rib.' " (Moses was traditionally thought to have
written the first five books of the Bible.)

Discrediting the rib story would not be unprecedented for a
Jewish writer of the first century. The erudite Philo Judeus of
Alexandria, a contemporary of Jesus who was not a Gnostic, said
the account of Eve coming from the rib of a man was "myth."
Philo asked rhetorically, "For how could anyone concede that a
woman or any person at all came into being out of a man's side?"
Yet, unlike Philo and his religiously skeptical audience, the Gnostic intellectuals were very religious—convinced of the reality of
the supernatural—and they reserved their skepticism for the traditional Jewish interpretations of Genesis.

The rib story was handled in yet another way in *On the Origin
of the World*, whose author seems to have known *Archons* or something similar. In *Origin*, Wisdom (Sophia) sent her daughter, Life
(Zoe), who is called "Eve," to raise Adam from the ground. She
does that, but the rulers see a problem here: Adam will realize
that Eve has divine power and knowledge greater than theirs.
In *Origin*, here is what the devious archons decided:

Let us not tell Adam, for he is not one of us. Rather let us bring a deep
sleep over him. And let us instruct him in his sleep to the effect that
she came from his rib, in order that his wife may obey, and he may be
lord over her.

In fact, the Genesis account of woman being created second

and from the flesh of man has long been cited in Christendom as a sign of male superiority. The Gnostic reversal of the relative importance of the male and female in the Garden may have contributed to an occasionally enlightened view of women in later Gnosticism. But at this time the prime intent of the reinterpretations was to discredit the Hebrew God and the conventional beliefs about him.

To resume the story: *The Hypostasis of the Archons* (and *Origin*) has Adam praise the spirit-endowed woman who is able to make Adam capable of standing up by her mere command, "Arise, Adam."

And when he (Adam) saw her, he said, "It is you who have given me life; you will be called 'Mother of the living.' For it is she who is my mother. It is she who is the physician, and the woman, and she who has given birth."

The stage is now set for the serpent. The "female spiritual principle" enters the snake, whom *Archons* calls "the instructor." The serpent-instructor tells the first couple that they were prohibited by the archons "out of envy" from eating from a certain tree. "Rather, your eyes shall open and you shall come to be like gods, recognizing evil and good." After this instruction, the divine feminine principle is removed from the snake, and the animal suffers the same fate as it did in Genesis—it is cursed and condemned to crawl everafter.

Not evident in English, or even in Greek, is what Yale's Bentley Layton calls "a series of learned puns in Aramaic on the root of *Hawwah*, the Aramaic equivalent of 'Eve' "—life, midwife, tree (of life), snake, and instructor. The play on words was pointedly used also in the midrash in *The Testimony of Truth*—the serpent "instructed" Eve and Eve "instructed" Adam. Rabbinical literature preserved a similar double entendre with Rabbi Aha speaking, as if addressing Eve, "The serpent was thy serpent, and thou art Adam's serpent."

Because the wordplays would have been most effective in Aramaic, Pearson says that the likeliest locale for the writings is Palestine or Syria. At the same time, Pearson notes that both Palestinian and Alexandrian Jewish speculation about the opening chapters of Genesis are present in *Archons* and *The Apocryphon of John.* Thus, the precise locale for this brand of Gnostic myth making is uncertain, but the religious matrix is clearly Jewish.

Somehow disillusioned by the Jewish faith, the Gnostic authors appear to be honestly bitter. It could be imagined that so much ridicule came from know-it-alls playing a game of story reversal to the hilt. The manuscripts mock the Creator—Yahweh, the God of Israel—turning to the language of field and village, Aramaic, for clever puns and crude names. For their principal heroine deities (Sophia, Pistis, Zoe) they often drew from the language of culture and philosophy, Greek.

Nevertheless, this revised view of primordial events offered an alternate philosophical solution to the problem of evil and suffering, and it was accepted as plausible by subsequent groups of Gnostics—and perhaps by the fourth-century Coptic Christians (either orthodox or heterodox) who laboriously copied the texts into leatherbound books.

10. The "Rape" of Eve and Norea the Ark Burner

Adam and his family and descendants are not uniformly depicted in the Nag Hammadi literature. Noah is a bad guy in one book, good guy in another. One consistent motif is that there are evil cosmic forces trying to capture the particles of spirit that show up occasionally on earth and in the Gnostic elect.

When the spirit-endowed woman in *The Hypostasis of the Archons* was able to raise Adam from the ground, the "authorities" (archons) became enamored of her.

"Come, let us sow our seed in her," they said as they pursued her.

But she "laughed at them for their witlessness and their blindness." While in their clutches she turned into a tree, but she left a resemblance of herself behind. The archons, in a gang rape, "defiled [it] foully."

Virtually the same episode is described in *On the Origin of the World*—the laughing Eve escapes the lustful archons by turning into a tree and leaving an imitation likeness behind. In *Origin*, Eve's counterfeit image bears all her children by the archons. But by a prearranged plan, says the author, resultant generations would contain the seed of light ultimately derived from the real Eve. Unknown to the evil cosmic rulers, their offspring would become "a hedge, or enclosure, for the light," an expression used twice in *Origin*.

A "hedge for the light" may mean about the same as a famous instruction the earliest rabbis said was passed down from Moses—"make a hedge for the Torah." To Jewish students of the Torah this meant "to keep the divine revelation from harm so that the sacred enclosure, so to speak, might always be free and open for the human to contemplate the divine," writes R. Travers Herford, in a commentary on the opening chapter of

Pirke Aboth. In the Gnostic scheme of things, humankind is the hedge not for the biblical revelations, but for the scattered particles of divine light that were not captured by the Creator God.

American scholar Orval Wintermute says the stance in *Origin* goes beyond simple commentary on Genesis to a theological position. Humans have a nature inherited from both the worldly archons and the highest light, if you accept the revised myths. "The primary task of man in the world is to repudiate the archons," Wintermute says. Humans need power from above to do it, but being half-breeds, they also mete out a peculiar justice by denouncing their makers, the archons.

The Apocryphon of John says the chief archon seduced Eve (but only after the divine spirit was removed from her) and she begat Eloim and Yave, animal-faced offspring, one unrighteous and the other righteous. The names are distortions of Elohim and Yahweh, the two names given to the God of Israel in Hebrew Scriptures! *The Apocryphon of John* says the chief archon gave the sons the names of Cain and Abel to deceive others.

The idea of heavenly powers mating with humans was not a Gnostic invention. Genesis 6 begins by saying "the sons of God," which scholars say refers to angels, took as their wives the fair daughters of men. The offspring "were the mighty men . . . of old, the men of renown." However, men became wicked and God was sorry he made humans. He saw favor in Noah only (Gen. 6:4–8).

True to the Gnostic tendency to reverse roles, *Archons* claims that humans were getting better. The archons decided to wipe out the humans with a flood, except for Noah and his children and the birds and the animals. Noah was told to build an ark.

Enter another heroine, Norea, the wife of Noah. She was unnamed in Genesis. According to *Archons*, Norea was also the virgin daughter of Eve. Noah bars his wife from entering the ark in *Archons*, so she blows against the craft and causes it to burn down. Noah builds another ship, but before his Norea has a chance to destroy it, the archons confront her.

"Your mother Eve came to us," they claimed.

Norea rebuts them, calling them the rulers of darkness. "You are accursed. And you did not know (sexually) my mother; instead it was your female counterpart that you knew. For I am not your descendant: rather, it is from the world above that I am come." (Only Cain, of Eve's children, was from the union of the chief archon and Eve. The rest were by Adam and Eve in *Archons*.)

The Archons turned black and demanded of her, "You must render service to us, as did your mother Eve." Norea cries for help from the highest God, and an angel with snowy white raiment descends, causing the archons to withdraw.

"Who are you?" asked Norea.

"It is I who am Eleleth, sagacity, the great angel who stands in the presence of the holy spirit. I have been sent to speak with you and save you from the grasp of the lawless. And I shall teach you about your root," said the angel.

Eleleth, identified in *The Apocryphon of John* as one of the four heavenly illuminators, tells Norea in *Archons* the story of how the world and the archons came into being after Sophia tried to procreate without a partner. The angel assures Norea that she and her children will be safe from the powers because her soul came from the incorruptible light.

The Apocryphon of John talks about the flood but not about Norea. Noah is a Gnostic hero in this book. He and the men of the "unwavering generation" are saved from Ialdabaoth's flood when they are hidden in a place, a "luminous cloud," while the earth is covered by darkness. *Apocryphon* again contradicts Genesis (7:7): "Not as Moses said, 'They hid themselves in an ark.'"

Norea is featured in another Nag Hammadi text, a very brief writing given the title *The Thought of Norea* because of its content. It mentions that she has "the four holy helpers who intercede on her behalf with the Father of the All" and who will help her regain her "place" in the celestial heights.

Many versions of the Norea story must have existed. The author of *Origin* refers readers to several other books for details on the various heavens and powers. Two texts he cites are "The First Book of Noraia" and "The First Logos of Noraia," which are not in the Nag Hammadi collection. Obviously, the heroine's name was variously spelled. Even *Archons* alternates between spelling it Norea and Orea.

According to Epiphanius, one group of Gnostics fabricated a book called *Noria*. The church father said these heretics claimed

Noria, Noah's wife, was barred from entering the ark, so she burned it down—not once, but *three* times.

Epiphanius said the Gnostics named Noah's wife Noria in an attempt to translate Pyrrha ("Fiery"), the flood heroine of Greek mythology, into an Aramaic name suggesting "fire." They were wrong, Epiphanius said, who claimed that Noah's real spouse was named Barthenos.

However, rabbinical sources said Noah's wife was named Naamah and was a descendant of Cain. She was saddled with a reputation of seductive wickedness in Jewish speculative circles. Naamah means "pleasing, lovely" in Hebrew. Pearson suggests that the Gnostics translated Naamah into the Greek for "pleasing, lovely," Horaia, and that word came also be spelled Orea and Norea.

For all of Norea's fiery charms, however, it is still Sophia who remains the most desirable heroine in primitive Gnostic religion. She is Wisdom, after all, sought by those in search of "gnosis," or knowledge. For the origins of the Gnostic Sophia, scholars have looked to Judaism. Her literary lineage stems from the wisdom literature in which Wisdom becomes personified. (Two feminine gender nouns for Wisdom were used—either the Hebrew "Hokhmah," as in the Old Testament's Proverbs, or "Sophia," the Greek equivalent used in Jewish apocryphal books such as the Wisdom of Solomon and Sirach.)

"Wisdom is radiant and unfading, and she is easily discerned by those who lover her, and is found by those who seek her" (Wisd. of Sol. 6:12). She is also pictured as a heavenly power existing from the beginning of time. "The Lord created me at the beginning of his work, the first of his acts of old," she says in Proverbs 8:22. "I dwelt in high places, and my throne was in a pillar of cloud," she declares in Sirach 24:4. "Alone I have made the circuit of the vault of heaven and have walked in the depths of the abyss" (24:5).

A wealth of imagery fed the wandering mind of the Gnostic. George MacRae identifies numerous parallels in comparing Wisdom in Jewish literature and Sophia in Gnostic writings. Beside the common heavenly abode, MacRae says both were linked with a Spirit, were instrumental in the creation of the world, strengthened Adam, communicated wisdom and revelations to humans, and descended into the ordinary world.

The Gnostic Sophia reascends to the light in texts such as *The Hypostasis of the Archons* and *On the Origin of the World.* That theme is generally absent in Jewish works because of the desire to show that Wisdom finds her home in Israel. "Cumulatively," MacRae says, "this long list of parallels between the Jewish Wisdom and the Gnostic Sophia makes it virtually impossible to rule out all influence of the former on the latter, and makes it at least probable that some kind of (no doubt perverse) use of the Jewish Wisdom figure lies at the source of the Gnostic myth."

Sometimes a single passage in Jewish wisdom literature seems capable of having prompted several Gnostic ideas. An example of Wisdom of Solomon 7:25: "For she [Wisdom] is a breath of the power of God, and a pure emanation of the glory of the Almighty; therefore nothing defiled gains entrance into her." The lustful archons attempted to "defile" the daughter of Sophia (Eve) but were tricked into raping her substitute image. Likewise, they were unsuccessful with the virgin granddaughter of Sophia (Norea).

The Gnostic Sophia is linked with the highest God and thereby could be considered a "pure emanation" of this God. But in some other, evidently later, treatises a Gnostic ambivalence develops toward Sophia. Gnostic believers must have been uncomfortable with the story line that has Sophia giving birth to the evil Creator God and to the debilitating world. How could a "pure emanation" of the highest God be responsible for all this evil?

Some Gnostics seemed to have resolved this by dividing the female deity in two, one a lofty figure and the other a fallen, deficient version. True to their individualistic ways, Gnostic myth makers differed in their descriptions:

In *The Apocryphon of John* a deity named Barbelo stands next to the Father, and Sophia operates on a lower level. The theology of the Gnostic Valentinus, according to church father Irenaeus, contained a higher and a lower Sophia. *The First Apocalypse of James* in the Nag Hammadi collection indicates that the "imperishable knowledge" is Sophia who is in the Father and the mother of Achamoth (a variant spelling of the Hebrew word for "wisdom"). This Achamoth is now the female Wisdom who tried to procreate without a partner but instead created the flawed cosmos. *The Gospel of Philip* says there are two Sophias: Echamoth, who is simply Sophia, and Echmoth, who is the Sophia of death. The process is clear, MacRae says: God's Wisdom is first personified in Gnostic writings, "then split, lest God's transcendence be compromised."

How did the *descent* of Wisdom in Jewish lore become the *fall* of Sophia in Gnosticism? MacRae suggests that the principal source was the error of Eve in the Garden. "Jewish tradition from biblical times onward had a keen sense of the disorder in the world resulting from the fall of the first couple" MacRae says. "Now the Gnostic, who began with a more radical notion that the world itself was disorder, would seek to explain this situation by postulating a fall in the (divine regions) of which the fall of man is but an inferior copy."

Although Jewish and Christian theology usually put the ultimate blame on Adam for the Fall, a plain reading of Genesis shows that the woman took the fruit, wanting to become wise, or as the serpent put it, to be "like God, knowing good and evil." This was Sophia's trouble too, said the Gnostics, because she wanted to give birth to something without a partner or to comprehend God—feats only possible by God.

"One would miss an essential insight into the Gnostic myths if he failed to realize that a close correspondence is intended there between the celestial world . . . and the material world of men," according to MacRae.

11. The Seed of Seth

The celestial Sophia and the courageous Eve and Norea were inspirational figures in a Gnostic conception of what transpired at the dawn of existence. The male hero for these Gnostics, the forerunner of their "unshakable race," is Seth, the third son of Adam.

After Cain slew Abel, according to Genesis (4:25), God provided Adam "another child instead of Abel." The Bible says little about Seth, a fact that prompted speculative Jewish faithful of two thousand years ago to fill in the gaps.

Legend held Seth to be a virtuous man whose descendants imitated his ways and lived happy, prosperous lives, says Josephus, writing in the late first century C.E. Josephus says that Seth's descendants discovered many things, including astrology. Jewish lore also said Adam predicted that great devastation lay ahead, so this knowledge was inscribed on two pillars, one of clay to survive a violent fire and the other of stone to resist a mighty flood.

Similar legendary features appear in the Nag Hammadi library's *The Apocalypse of Adam*, which was written as if it were the deathbed revelations and apocalyptic prophecies of Adam to his son Seth. Of course, the usual Gnostic twist appears in this version, which opens with Adam, in his seven-hundredth year, saying:

Listen to my words, my son Seth. When God had created me out of the earth along with Eve your mother, I went about with her in a glory which she had seen in the aeon from which we had come forth. She taught me a word of knowledge of the eternal God. And we resembled the great eternal angels, for we were higher than the God who had created us.

Here are familiar themes—Eve was an instructor to Adam and the two of them were superior to the Creator God. *The Apocalypse of Adam* continues to say that this God gave vent to his wrath on

Adam and Eve, causing their glory and knowledge to leave them. "And we served him in fear and slavery," says Adam. The hitherto unknown *Apocalypse of Adam* stands in sharp contrast to a faithfully Jewish, non-Gnostic writing that survived through the centuries, *The Life of Adam and Eve*, in which the two regret their sins in Paradise. It is considered a first-century C.E. writing.

Because of "its massive dependence on Jewish traditions" and "its lack of obvious Christian influence," Pearson says *The Apocalypse of Adam* is a "test case" for the argument for the existence of Gnostic beliefs arising out of a Jewish and non-Christian setting. The lack of Christian influence is a disputed point, but Pearson appears to be among the majority who say it is either devoid of Christian touches or that what little exists is simply a later addition. The scholarly debate over *The Apocalypse of Adam* and related texts has been a major one in Nag Hammadi studies, and not without good reason.

Such distinctions are needed to estimate the period of composition. That in turn offers the potential for new clues to the course of Western religious history at a crucial turning point. In other words, were the virulent critics of the Creator simply Jews-turned-Christians cutting their ties in a nasty fashion? Early Christian groups all seemed to honor the God of Israel with the exception of the followers of the second-century radical Marcion, who rejected the Hebrew Bible and was denounced by the church as a heretic. Or were they sincerely disenchanted Jews in a religious revolt, unprecedented for Jews but conceivable during a period of major transition for Judaism? Such a revolt surely would have been overshadowed by the Roman destruction of the Jerusalem Temple in 70 C.E. and the forced dispersal of Jews. Led by prominent rabbis, Judaism moved to define its canon of Scripture and steadily assembled rabbinic rulings on what it meant to be Jewish.

If Christianity and Gnosticism developed out of Judaism separately and at roughly the same time, the possibilities are obvious for the cross-fertilization of two new religions, each struggling to be the more persuasive.

Before returning to *The Apocalypse of Adam*, we need to place it into its broader Gnostic context. *The Apocalypse of Adam* is considered to be one of eleven works in the Nag Hammadi library that were produced by a sect of Sethian Gnostics. Following mainly the pioneering studies in the early 1970s by Hans-Martin Schenke and colleagues, scholars count ten other works in that literature: *The Apocryphon of John*, *The Hypostasis of the Archons*, *The Gospel of the Egyptians*, *The Three Steles of Seth*, *Zostrianos*, *Melchizedek*, *The Thought of Norea*, *Marsanes*, *Allogenes*, and *The Trimorphic Protennoia*.

They share "a complex of interconnected basic beliefs and basic concepts," Schenke says. References to a baptismal rite, sometimes called "the five seals," has suggested to some that the movement originated among Jewish baptizing sects. The name "Seth" does not appear in all the Sethian writings. More than simply a personage of the past, Seth is regarded as a heavenly figure. The Sethian "system," loosely speaking, at times sees him as a coming savior. When a Sethian writing has obvious Christian influences, Christ tends to be identified with Seth or Adam.

Indeed, Epiphanius, a bishop in Cyprus who wrote about heretical groups circa 375 C.E., said he knew of Sethians from personal encounters and written accounts. Epiphanius said Sethians traced their descent from Seth and glorify him, and "they even call him Christ and assert that he is Jesus."

Most of the Sethian Gnostic writings in the Nag Hammadi library were probably composed between 100 and 250 C.E., estimates John D. Turner. But the University of Nebraska professor also believes Sethianism originated as a non-Christian sect during the first centuries B.C.E. and C.E.

Although it is only hinted at in *The Apocalypse of Adam* and *The Hypostasis of the Archons*, the Sethian heavens typically teem with divine entities, all named and enumerated. The highest heavenly beings form a Father-Mother-Son triad—but it is not usually stated so plainly. The complicated network of otherworldly beings reveals the impact of Greek philosophy deriving ultimately from Plato. As in Neoplatonic philosophy, "Thought," "Word" and other abstract concepts are emanations of the deity and play a role in the primordial drama. Researchers are unsure when Greek metaphysics blended with the Sethian revision of Jewish lore, but Turner suggests that it happened during the late first century C.E. and throughout the second and third centuries.

Not every piece of writing bearing the name Seth is necessarily classified as Sethian in origin. The Nag Hammadi library also contains *The Second Treatise of the Seth*, but the name Seth only occurs in the title—it is a writing about Jesus Christ. Nevertheless, the treatise shares some ideas, names, and motifs with Sethian works.

The Paraphrase of Shem, a clearly non-Christian composition in the Nag Hammadi copy, was apparently available to the church father Hippolytus in a Christianized form, which he called "The Paraphrase of Seth." Nag Hammadi's *Paraphrase of Shem* has three primeval roots—Light, Darkness, and Spirit—revealed to Shem as he is caught up into heaven. Although *The Paraphrase of Shem* is extremely difficult to follow, its importance lies primarily in its witness as a non-Christian Gnostic writing with an interest in reinterpreting Jewish themes. It "uses and radically transforms Old Testament materials, especially from Genesis," says Frederick Wisse. Shem is told, for example, that Sodom "will be burned unjustly."

Another non-Christian work that scholars say does fall into the Sethian Gnostic classification is *The Three Steles of Seth*, who is described in it as "the father of the living and unshakable race." The document presents three prayers to accompany a heavenly ascent that were supposedly preserved on three steles, or stone tablets. The prayers are successively to Geradamas (the Son), Barbelo (the Mother), and the supreme Father—all of whom are given numerous attributes, including the Neoplatonic triad of Mind-Life-Existence, respectively.

"The Jewish and Sethian liturgical background of the tractate is remarkably merged with Neoplatonic philosophical terminology," says James M. Robinson. The same vocabulary is found in *Zostrianos* and *Allogenes*. These two Sethian writings were listed in the Neoplatonist *Life of Plotinus* and were refuted by Plotinus's school. The Sethian Gnostic appropriation of Neoplatonic philosophy and Christian motifs drew fire from both camps.

In *The Apocalypse of Adam*, however, the author's familiarity with and focus on Jewish speculation of the first century C.E. is striking. Adam receives his revelation from three heavenly beings, a literary device similar to the visions from angels in Jewish apocalyptic works. Just as Eve in *The Life of Adam and Eve* says God will bring two disasters on humans—by water and by fire (which Jewish readers would understand as a reference to the great flood and to the destruction of Sodom and Gomorrah), just so *The Apocalypse of Adam* has Adam prophesy the two God-wrought calamities of flood waters and of fire, sulphur, and asphalt. Adam also predicts a third and final judgment against humans, but Pearson and Pheme Perkins of Boston College note that a threefold judgment already existed in non-Gnostic Jewish traditions, notably in *1 Enoch*.

The Apocalypse of Adam says that the men of knowledge will be saved from the flood by great angels who will bring them "into the place where the spirit [of] life dwells." God intends to save only Noah, his family, and the creatures with an ark. When God spies a whole generation of (Gnostic) men who escaped the flood, God accuses Noah of creating another generation "so that you might scorn my power." But Noah pleads innocence. Later, four hundred thousand descendants of two of Noah's sons defect and join the seed of Seth and enjoy the blessings of that association. Those who stayed loyal complain to God, here called "Sakla," one of three derogatory names in Sethian works. The Hebrew deity answers with the fiery judgment, but the angels Abrasax, Sablo, and Gamaliel descend to rescue these men and take them to an aeon far above the archons. "The God of Israel and those faithful to him are mocked," observes Perkins, who says the author engages in "deliberate irony" by mimicking Jewish literary styles.

Adam then speaks of "the illuminator of knowledge" who will save from "the day of death" those peoples who "reflect upon the knowledge of the eternal God" (not the lower, wrathful God). The illuminator, Adam says, "will perform signs and wonders in order to scorn the powers and their ruler."

Disturbed, the God of the powers will ask, "What is the power of this man who is higher than we?" The illuminator's "glory" will withdraw to holy houses, but the powers will not see this. "Then they will punish the flesh of the man upon whom the holy spirit came," Adam says.

A few studies have claimed that the latter passage is a veiled reference to Jesus. But Pearson contends that the passage, in context, follows "a pre-Christian Jewish literary pattern dealing with the earthly persecution and subsequent exaltation of the righteous man."

Likewise, MacRae says he finds no explicit or veiled Christian allusions in *The Apocalypse of Adam*. He feels that the tribulation of the illuminator was drawn from the images of the suffering servant in Isaiah, an Old Testament image that Christians also employed to describe Jesus. "The point is that the early Christian preaching did not invent the notion of a suffering religious leader out of whole cloth," MacRae says.

Three names invoked at the very end of *The Apocalypse of Adam* are Yesseus, Mazareus, and Yessedekeus, which have looked to some like distortions of Jesus of Nazareth. The same names appear twice in *The Gospel of the Egyptians*, which underwent Christian editing. Pearson suggests that they are more likely mystical names of Seth than references to Jesus.

Such claims that some Nag Hammadi writings totally lack any Christian touches probably would have been disputed more fiercely if it were not for two treatises in the collection that are very similar, yet very different. Though they are not Sethian texts, they illustrate the Christianizing process. They are *Eugnostos the Blessed* and *The Sophia of Jesus Christ*.

—*Eugnostos the Blessed* is a non-Christian "letter" to followers from one Eugnostos. He expounds on the existence of an invisible realm of the Father and three principal beings, each androgynous, or male-female, despite their names: the Father's image, Immortal Man; Immortal Man's son, Son of Man, and Son of Man's son, simply called the Savior. Compounding the gender contradictions, Sophia appears as the "female aspect," or consort, of some of these supposedly androgynous beings.

—*The Sophia of Jesus Christ* presents virtually the same teaching and in the same order, but it is recast in the form of responses by the risen Christ to questions from his disciples. The "Savior" is identified now as Christ and has a more significant role to save people enslaved by the powers of the lower heavens.

In Codex III, *The Sophia of Jesus Christ* immediately follows *Eugnostos the Blessed*. At the end of the latter, it is predicted that one will come who will speak the words written by Eugnostos "joyously and in pure knowledge."

Like the ancient scribe who wrote that, modern scholars recognize that *Eugnostos* presents the earlier format of the treatise, namely, something written without any trace of Christian influence.* Few scholars argue the reverse—that *Eugnostos* was produced by de-Christianizing *The Sophia of Jesus Christ.*

Why was the original non-Christian writing turned into *The Sophia of Jesus Christ?* Parrott guesses: "To express newly acquired Christian beliefs or to attract Christians to Gnostic teachings, or perhaps for both reasons."

The thesis of a Jewish setting for Gnostic origins, advocated by few before the Nag Hammadi discovery, has found many leading advocates—scholars who also acknowledge that ideas from Greek philosophy abetted the mocking attack on the Hebrew God. At the same time, some scholars are not convinced that Gnostic religion developed outside of Christian circles.

One such scholar prominent in Gnostic studies is Bentley Layton, professor of ancient Christian history at Yale University. Layton, who was part of the Claremont project to publish the Nag Hammadi library, also organized and directed the International Conference on Gnosticism at Yale in 1978, which resulted in a two-volume work.

And in *The Gnostic Scriptures* (1987), Layton combined his translations of more than a dozen Nag Hammadi writings with selections from previously known Gnostic works and church father polemics against Gnostic sects. Layton included Hermetic writings under the Gnostic umbrella and frequently eschewed conventional translations for Nag Hammadi library titles, even preferring to designate the discovery site in Upper Egypt as Pbou (or Pabau, today called Faw Qibli, where the ruins are still visible of the basilica of St. Pachomius). His individualistic approach notwithstanding, Layton provides an updated overview of Gnostic myths and provocative theories of how Gnostic schools of thought spread through the Mediterranean and Near East.

Layton wrote in his book that the texts discovered in 1945

---

*A second copy of *Eugnostos* is in Codex V and a copy of *The Sophia of Jesus Christ* exists in the Berlin collection of four Gnostic texts found in 1896. The Codex III copies were used for the side-by-side translations printed in *The Nag Hammadi Library in English,* but the other copies proved useful to translator-editor Douglas M. Parrott because three pages were missing from the Codex III versions.

which lack obvious Christian elements do not amount to conclusive evidence of a pre- or non-Christian branch of the Gnostic
movement. "Ancient Christians certainly made use of writings
that contained no explicit references to Jesus Christ or to other
distinctive marks of their own religion," Layton says, citing the
Old Testament as an example.

Layton suggests that Gnostic beliefs arose out of Platonic
myths of creation combined with the book of Genesis. He continues:

> Speculation of this kind—from the period of "Middle Platonism"—was
> popular with learned Greek-speaking Jews of Alexandria at the time of
> Philo Judaeus (ca. 30 B.C.–ca. A.D. 45). Such speculation was also fash-
> ionable in pagan philosophical circles of the first and second centuries
> A.D., and beyond. Since the gnostic myth seems to presuppose this spec-
> ulative tradition, it *might* be as old as Philo Judaeus. Yet nothing proves
> that it *must* be so old.

Nevertheless, another scholar long active in Nag Hammadi
studies believes the discovery of non-Christian Gnostic manuscripts spelled the end for the theory of Christian origins. He is
Charles W. Hedrick, a veteran of the Nag Hammadi publishing
effort who did his doctoral dissertation under Robinson at Claremont.

While teaching religious studies at Southwest Missouri State
University, Hedrick cosponsored the Working Seminar on Gnosticism and Early Christianity at Springfield, Missouri, in 1983,
resulting in a book published in 1986. In his introduction to that
book, Hedrick writes:

> Because the library does contain several gnostic texts that show no ev-
> idence of having been influenced by Christianity (*The Apocalypse of Adam,
> The Paraphrase of Shem, The Three Steles of Seth*, and *Eugnostos*), it dem-
> onstrates beyond question that gnosticism was not simply a Christian
> heresy. For further support one may also point to other originally non-
> Christian texts that were later appropriated for Christian gnosticism
> through a sometimes extremely thin veneer of Christianizing: *The Gospel
> of the Egyptians, The Apocryphon of John, The Hypostasis of the Archons* and
> *The Trimorphic Protennoia*. While there may be no extant gnostic manu-
> scripts from the early first century C.E. to show that there existed a pre-
> Christian gnosticism in a *chronological* sense, these texts clearly dem-
> onstrate the existence of a pre-Christian gnosticism in an *ideological*

sense. Such hard evidence presents a previously unavailable avenue for investigating the interaction between Christianity and its gnostic opponents. They provide concrete sources not only for studying a gnosticism uninfluenced by Christianity but they also give us an insight into the influence of Christianity upon gnosticism, and gnosticism upon Christianity.

Just how Gnostic myths, especially the Sethian variety, may have influenced Christianity is discussed in the next chapter.

12. The Gnostic Redeemers

Few Christians would object to a claim that occasionally the New Testament describes Jesus as the voice or embodiment of the Jewish scriptural figure of Wisdom. After all, the Gospels declare Jesus "fulfilled" the Old Testament in many ways, especially as the anticipated Messiah.

But it might be controversial to suggest that Jesus was also glorified as a heaven-sent redeemer under the influence of a Gnostic redeemer myth. An instinctive and traditional church response would be that Christ was described as a preexisting savior who descended to earth and returned to heaven simply because in fact that is what happened, according to the Bible. However, "the more critical thinker might ask where that religious symbolism comes from," as one scholar put it.

Before the Nag Hammadi discovery, the Gnostic redeemer theories of Rudolf Bultmann and others were attacked because this alleged myth was reconstructed from evidence in the New Testament and from religious texts of a much later date. But it wasn't long after critical studies began on the Sethian Gnostic documents from Nag Hammadi that "the missing documentation" appeared, as James M. Robinson asserts. At least two texts were touted as providing evidence of the Gnostic redeemer myth—*The Apocalypse of Adam* and *The Trimorphic Protennoia*.

In *The Apocalypse of Adam* "we have a clearly developed redeemer-myth which is at once Gnostic and without any reference to Jesus as the Gnostic redeemer or his prototype," George MacRae wrote in a 1965 article. The redeemer in *Adam* is the illuminator of knowledge, who is understood also to be the heavenly Seth. When he appears to perform "signs and wonders" to scorn the powers led by the lower God, the wrathful deity punishes the flesh of the bodily form that Seth had taken as a disguise.

Jesus, of course, is presented in the New Testament Gospels as performing miracles and causing a stir, yet not being recognized as a divine figure by the earthly authorities. He is killed, but he survives and eventually ascends to heaven. The apostle Paul, writing to the Corinthian church before the Gospels were composed, uses the imagery of the savior going unidentified by malevolent cosmic powers. Saying that the church teaches a secret wisdom decreed before the ages by God, Paul adds: "None of the rulers of this age [literally, "archons" of this "aeon"] understood this; for if they had, they would not have crucified the Lord of glory" (1 Cor. 2:8). New Testament writers also expected the heavenly Christ to return in what they believed was the fast-approaching end times.

The Sethian myth speaks of three comings. *Adam* says that angels rescued the seed of Seth from the flood and the fire, but then says the illuminator (Seth) will come by "for the third time" to rescue souls from the final destruction.

Indeed, *The Apocryphon of John* and *The Trimorphic Protennoia* both "use a scheme in which the revealer descends into the world three times. The first two cause destruction in chaos," Perkins says. By coming in human form the third time, the revealer avoids these circumstances, she says.

(A revealer-redeemer figure in the non-Christian *Paraphrase of Shem* also fools the powers of darkness by "putting on the beast," apparently the body, in his work of salvation. Wisse proposed in 1970 that *The Paraphrase of Shem* contains elements of the Gnostic redeemer myth. Because the text's narrative is incoherent at times, however, a discussion of the Sethian redeemer is more useful here.)

The persistent question of those familiar with the Jesus story, however, is whether the Sethian Gnostics were influenced by Christian lore to predict that their savior, Seth, would come, undergo persecution, and yet triumph much in the way Jesus was said to have done. And, again, a few phrases in *The Apocalypse of Adam* sound "Christian." Yet they were not expressions introduced by Christianity. The illuminator is predicted to perform "signs and wonders," but that was a common phrase in Jewish literature. Wisdom withstood the dread kings with signs and wonders in the Wisdom of Solomon (10:16). Adam also predicts that those whom the illuminator saves "will receive his name upon the water." But that could be expected in a baptizing sect like the Sethians, who attached importance to learning secret names.

Whenever Gnostics used Christian ideas, they were obvious about it, MacRae argues. "They deliberately wish[ed] to incorporate Christian or Jewish figures or even representatives of classical and other mythologies to show that the 'best' of other traditions were in reality Gnostic," he wrote in 1972. But in *Adam* distinctive Christian wording is absent.

Another Nag Hammadi manuscript, *The Concept of Our Great Power*, might appear to ruin that argument, but MacRae says it doesn't. "This text contains a comparatively detailed account of the future coming of Jesus without any trace of Christian names," he said. But the New Testament story of Jesus is definitely used here: the coming one "will speak in parables" and will be "betrayed" by "one of those who followed him," and his "word annulled the law of the age."

As for a Gnostic impact on early Christianity, some scholars cautiously pointed in the 1970s to possible indirect influence on New Testament authors writing in the last quarter of the first century C.E. and early in the next. In one unusual section of *The Apocalypse of Adam*, thirteen erroneous stories of the coming of the illuminator and one correct one are told. In 1970, Robinson wrote about some striking similarities between these birth, baptism, and epiphany scenes in *Adam*, the Jesus baptism scenes in the Gospel of Mark and the apocryphal *Gospel of the Hebrews*, and a mythological birth narrative in Revelation 12.

These similarities demonstrate—at the minimum—the wealth of apocalyptic expectations and spiritual concepts in texts circulating at the time of Jesus, many of them lost forever. Rather than claiming that one text borrowed directly from another, scholars tend to say that texts with similarities may have borrowed from common oral or written sources. A *close-matching* parallel can point to the use of a source behind the New Testament.

That was the case when the East Berlin Nag Hammadi team published the thesis in 1973 that *The Trimorphic Protennoia* might contain a genuine parallel to the prologue of the Gospel of John (1:1–18). The Coptic version of *The Trimorphic Protennoia* in Codex XIII retains the Greek title, which means "First Thought in Three Forms." Protennoia is the first thought of the ineffable Father and makes three descents to the world as redeemer, appearing first as Father, second as Mother, and third as Son. In her last descent, she is also called the "Word"—thus the inevitable comparisons with the opening of John.

A member of the East Berlin team, Gesine Schenke, published the first translation of the text in 1974 and enlarged on the group's thesis by suggesting that the statements by Protennoia stand "in their natural context." By contrast, she said, their parallels in the prologue of John appear to artificially serve a purpose alien to them. From that point, she said the scholarly debate often degenerated into alternate claims that one text depended directly on the other. Some said the Gnostic text, which has undergone minor Christian additions, must have been inspired by the Gospel of John.

MacRae disagreed with that counterthesis. The Jesuit scholar, who chaired the Sethian section of the international symposium at Yale in 1978, summarized the discussions with what he termed "the heart of the argument":

In any case, it is easier to envisage the spread of the relevant attributes in the Gnostic work as original, than to suppose that the author dismantled the narrowly focused Prologue of the Fourth Gospel to spread the attributes throughout a much broader mythological context. It is important to note here that no one seriously argues that the Fourth Gospel is indebted to the Nag Hammadi tractate as to a literary work. Clearly both are dependent on developments in the wisdom tradition and may simply have had a common ancestor. But whether that ancestor is already a Gnostic modification of the wisdom tradition is the question at stake.

The Gnostic character of *The Trimorphic Protennoia* itself is undisputed. The threefold descent of the redeemer is typical of some other Sethian works. Not only that, Protennoia has embraced the role of Seth, for in the course of her revelation Protennoia (a feminine noun) speaks repeatedly of her children, who are also called her "seed." She also brings the baptism of the "five seals."

Ultimately, the "Word" in the Gnostic text and in John both assume aspects of Lady Wisdom found in Proverbs, who was with

God always and took part in Creation. Wisdom descended to earth; some were receptive, others not.

The decisive parallels between John's prologue (1:1–18) and *Protennoia* lie in the three stages of activity in each of the two texts. The parallels:

—Protennoia discloses her preexistence with the Father and her pervasive creative activity. Second, she arrives in the world to bring knowledge to humans. People who perceive her call belong to the "children of light whose father I am," thus making children of God of those who "accept" this gift. And third, as the "Word," she comes down "to the world of mortals" to redeem all her "brethren."

—In John's prologue, the Word was not only with God in the beginning but was God and "all things were made through him" (1:3). Second, the prologue speaks of the light coming into the world, "yet the world knew him not" (1:10). "But to all who received him, who believed in his name, he gave power to become children of God" (1:12). Third, the Word becomes flesh, but retaining his glory, to bring grace to humans (1:14–17).

The Trimorphic Protennoia depicts, at great length, the whole issue of salvation in three dramatic periods. The three-stage drama is a common Sethian trait, but it is not a New Testament view of religious history. At the Yale symposium, Robinson inferred from this that "the traces in the Prologue of John of periodizing, namely the Logos being in the primordial period, in the pre-Christian 'spermatic' period and in the incarnate period, would then become intelligible as the way in which that non-Christian tradition was adapted and unified in Christ." More precisely, the source used by the Gospel's prologue was probably already a Gnostic modification of the wisdom tradition, according to Robinson, Hans-Martin Schenke, and others.

That research was summarized at the 1987 meeting of the Society of Biblical Literature in a paper that elaborated on other parallels pointing to the Gnostic myth as the common ground. Both the Gnostic redeemer and the hymnic representation of Jesus describe the Word as "light." By bringing knowledge, the prologue's Word lightens the darkness. Similarly, Protennoia as Word is the cosmic light "who was sent to illuminate those who dwell in the darkness," the paper's author noted.

Futhermore, the sudden switch to "we" in the prologue, beginning with verse 14, could suggest that a baptismal experience is being confessed—"we have seen" the glory and "we have received" grace. Only hinted at in John, baptism forms a major reason, the paper observed, for the descent by Protennoia, including the disclosure of passwords to get past cosmic rulers on one's way to the highest heaven. In the Gnostic text, a point occurs where the Word is praised—"He is the light that dwells in the light"—followed by the collective confession, "We alone are those whom thou hast redeemed from the visible world, in that we have been saved."

In conclusion, the paper said *The Trimorphic Protennoia* provides the best evidence for the Gnostic religious symbolism employed at the start of the Gospel of John—"Jewish wisdom speculation has passed through this Gnostic filter before reaching the Prologue itself."

The author of the paper was Gesine Robinson, who first suggested the connection thirteen years earlier as Gesine Schenke, at the time married to Hans-Martin Schenke. After a divorce, she was remarried, in 1986, to James Robinson, who was also previously married.

III. THE JESUS OF HERESY

13. The Laughing Savior

The disciple Peter has a perplexing vision in *The Apocalypse of Peter*, a Nag Hammadi text composed by an anonymous Christian Gnostic probably in the second century C.E. While talking with the Savior, Peter suddenly says he is having a vision of people taking Jesus away. Peter becomes unnerved, because next he seems to see two Jesuses on the cross.

"Who is the one glad and laughing on the tree?" Peter asks, referring to the wooden cross. "And is it another one whose feet and hands they are striking?"

The Savior interprets the prophetic vision to Peter: "He whom you saw on the tree, glad and laughing, this is the living Jesus. But this one into whose hands and feet they drive the nails is his fleshly part, which is the substitute being put to shame, the one who came into being in his likeness."

Further, the Savior "stands joyfully looking at those who did him violence. . . . He laughs at their lack of perception, knowing that they are born blind."

The Jesus who laughs at his would-be crucifiers is one of the most unusual interpretations in Christian annals. The story is found in another Nag Hammadi text as well. Until the manuscript windfall from upper Egypt the story was known only from an account by Irenaeus, a bishop writing in the late second century.

The stories were no laughing matter for leaders of what became orthodox Christianity. It was heresy, they said, to teach that Jesus escaped the crucifixion by shedding his body. When certain Christian Gnostics and others took a modified view that Jesus was indeed crucified yet didn't suffer, that theological offense was called Docetism. Pointing to the emphasis on the suffering and physical death of Jesus in the New Testament Gospels, church leaders insisted that Jesus was no less human for all of his divinity.

Not all Christian Gnostics thought alike on the issue, as evidenced by Nag Hammadi texts. Several treatises are ambiguous on Jesus' suffering. Some treat the issue with sophisticated theological arguments. One exceptional tractate asserts the physical nature of Jesus in no uncertain terms.

The oldest full-scale church polemic against Gnostic sects was written by Irenaeus, who became the bishop of Lyons in 177–178. His main work was "Exposure and Refutation of the Falsely So-called Gnosis" in five books. It survived in full only in Latin and is generally known by the abbreviated Latin title, *Adversus Haereses (Against Heresies)*. Irenaeus's purpose was admittedly "not only to expose but also from every side to wound the beast" that had penetrated the faith.

The bishop described a "laughing Jesus" account, which he said was taught by Basilides, a Gnostic teacher active in Alexandria in the period between 117 and 138 C.E. Irenaeus wrote that Basilides had a system of 365 heavens, the lowest one headed by the conquest-minded God of the Jews. The Father, seeing the plight of other nations, sent his Nous, or "Mind," who was also called Christ, to free people from the power of those who made the world. Basilides said Christ appeared on earth as a man and performed miracles, according to Irenaeus.

For the same reason also he did not suffer, but a certain Simon of Cyrene was compelled to carry his cross for him; and this (Simon) was transformed by him (Jesus) so that he was thought to be Jesus himself, and was crucified through ignorance and error. Jesus, however, took on the form of Simon, and stood by laughing at them.

For since he was an incorporeal power and the Nous of the unborn Father, he was transformed in whatever way he pleased, and in this way he ascended to him who had sent him, laughing at them, since he could not be held and was invisible to all.

Irenaeus said that Basilides taught that if one professes belief in the crucified Jesus, "he is still a slave, and under the power of those who made the bodies." Not only that, Basilides criticized those who revered the prophets and the law in Hebrew Scriptures—"the prophecies came from the rulers who made the world, and . . . the law in particular came from their chief, him who led the people out of the land of Egypt," according to Irenaeus.

In Nag Hammadi's *Second Treatise of the Great Seth*, a crucifixion account is similar to the alleged story of Basilides only in that Simon of Cyrene (see Mark 15:21) is mentioned. Christ, here a preexisting heavenly being, speaks throughout in the first person. In explaining his apparent suffering and death, the heavenly revealer said he was "not afflicted at all" and "did not die in reality." Alluding next to gospel descriptions of Jesus' Passion, the revealer says:

It was another, their father, who drank the gall and the vinegar; it was not I. They struck me with the reed; it was another, Simon, who bore the cross on his shoulder. It was another upon whom they placed the crown of thorns. But I was rejoicing in the height over the wealth of the archons and the offspring of their error, of their empty glory. And I was laughing at their ignorance.

The writer does not really say that Simon was crucified by mistake. The vague implication is that other bodies were punished and it only seemed to the "blind" archons that Christ suffered and died.

The mocking attitude pervading the text extends to the Jewish biblical authorities, who are all called "laughingstocks" in a litany of ridicule. "Adam was a laughingstock, since he was made a counterfeit type of man by the Hebdomad (seventh heaven), as if he had become stronger than I and my brothers. We are innocent with respect to him, since we have not sinned." The revealer proceeds to name as laughingstocks in turn Abraham, Isaac, Jacob, David, Solomon, "the twelve prophets," Moses, and finally the Archon. None of them—and not even John the Baptist—"knew me or my brothers," the narrator says. Earlier, the narrator said that when the head archon, called Yaldabaoth, boasted that he was God and no other existed beside him, "I laughed joyfully when I examined his empty glory."

At the conclusion of *The Second Treatise of the Great Seth*, the narrator says, "I alone am the friend of Sophia. I have been in the bosom of the Father from the beginning, in the place of the sons of the truth." Although the writing is not counted among the Nag Hammadi works composed by Sethian Gnostics, the text shows many signs of having been influenced by them, despite the fact that the name Seth goes unmentioned in the body of the writing.

In neither *The Apocalypse of Peter* nor *The Second Treatise of the Great Seth* are the Jews or Romans accused of unjustly condemning Jesus to death. The New Testament accounts of the Jewish trial and cries of the crowd to crucify Jesus contributed to Christian anti-Semitism through the centuries, according to today's Jewish-Christian studies. But the Christian Gnostics blamed the crucifixion on the evil powers who enslave unknowing people and force them to do their bidding.

That does not mean the Christian Gnostics ignored real-life religious opponents. The authors of the two texts had their Christ figure denounce contemporary critics, which may have included both orthodox churches and competing sects. The *Second Treatise* hints at persecution from "those who think they are advancing the name of Christ, since they are unknowingly empty, not knowing who they are, like dumb animals." *The Apocalypse of Peter* has the Savior predict to Peter that there will be outsiders "who name themselves bishop and also deacons, as if they have received their authority from God. They bend themselves under the judgment of the leaders. Those people are dry canals."

One more text relevant to the laughing reaction to the cross is *The Acts of John*. An apocryphal work dated as possibly third century, C.E., it is only mildly Gnostic and only obliquely critical of orthodox churches, which is perhaps why about 70 percent of it survived in various translations through time.

When John cannot bear to watch Jesus apparently suffer on the cross, the disciple flees to a cave and weeps. But then "the Lord" appears in shining form and says, "John, for the people below in Jerusalem I am being crucified and pierced with lances and reeds and given vinegar and gall to drink. But to you I am speaking, and listen to what I speak."

John is given a vision of "the Lord himself above the cross," having no shape but only a kind of sweet voice. The Lord then proceeds to tell John more about the contradictory nature of his divinity, advising John to "ignore the many and despise those who are outside the mystery." After the Lord had completed his revelation, he was taken up into heaven unseen by any of the multitude. Going down from his cave on the Mount of Olives, John said, "I laughed at them all, since he had told me what they had said about him." John laughs, not Jesus, but it appears to be a toned-down rendition of the story known to Irenaeus and two Nag Hammadi texts.

In one sense, the Christian Gnostic story of Jesus mocking his persecutors reverses the accounts in Mark, Matthew, and Luke. In Mark, for instance, the soldiers "mock" Jesus (15:20) and so do the chief priests (15:31). Jesus himself does not "laugh" or "mock" in the New Testament Gospels, notwithstanding the modern attempts to show the humor of Jesus in the Gospels. Luke has Jesus say in his Sermon on the Plain, "Blessed are you that weep now, for you shall laugh" (6:21) and "Woe to you that laugh now, for you shall mourn and weep" (6:25). Similar promises of an end to sorrow appear in Matthew 5:4 and John 16:20, 22. The inspiration for the Christian Gnostic image of Jesus evading and laughing at his enemies was probably not the New Testament crucifixion accounts, but rather the content and tenor of Sethian stories.

Strikingly similar to the crucifixion escape is the story of the spirit-imbued Eve in *The Hypostasis of the Archons*, who was pursued by archons attempting to rape her. She laughed at their blindness. She eluded them by turning into a tree and the archons raped instead Eve's substitute form.

The mocking attitude was also present in *The Apocalypse of Adam*, which pointed to the final coming of the illuminator, who "will perform signs and wonders in order to scorn the powers and their ruler."

Robert M. Grant suggests that the laughing Jesus may have been inspired by Psalm 2, which was held to be meaningful by early Christians. It says, starting at verse 2: "The kings of the earth set themselves, and the rulers take counsel together, against the Lord and his anointed." But "he who sits in the heavens laughs; the Lord has them in derision" (Ps. 2:4).

Another formative image could have been Wisdom. She is a would-be savior in the first chapter of Proverbs for those who listen. She is a "laughing savior," in fact. "How long will scoffers delight in their scoffing and fools hate knowledge?" she asks (1:22). For those who continue, she says, "I . . . will laugh at your calamity; I will mock when panic strikes you . . ." (1:26).

The Docetic view in Gnostic Christian writings was not always tied to the image of a laughing savior. *The First Apocalypse of James* depicts the brother of Jesus anguished over news of Jesus' crucifixion and praying on a mountain. But "the Lord" appears to James and assures him, "I am he who was within me. Never have I suffered in any way, nor have I been distressed." The Lord tells James also that the people who crucified him should not be judged, for they were the tools of the archons. The Lord said that his earthly reappearance will be intended "as a reproof to the archons."

One consequence of the Gnostic position that Jesus was just a human form assumed temporarily by the divine savior was that Christian Gnostics had to deny the rather substantial tradition that Jesus had flesh-and-blood brothers. Mark 6:3 names four brothers, including James. Paul refers to the privileged "brothers of the Lord" (1 Cor. 9:5) and to James of Jerusalem specifically as "the brother of the Lord" (Gal. 1:19). But James is told by the Lord in *The First Apocalypse of James* that "you are not my brother materially." And *The Second Apocalypse of James*, also in the Nag Hammadi collection, indicates James is a "relative," perhaps a stepbrother. Ironically, those positions coincided with orthodox doctrine developing in the second century that James, Judas, and other brothers were not really brothers. The doctrine arose in order to say that Mary, the mother of Jesus, was perpetually a virgin. The second-century solution, still held by Eastern Orthodox churches, was that Jesus' siblings must have been stepbrothers from a previous marriage by Joseph.

Christian Gnostics sometimes could repeat rather traditional creeds about the crucifixion and yet interpret it in ways differently from the orthodox. Peter recites a creed in *The Letter of Peter to Philip* that would seem to echo the New Testament emphasis on Jesus' corporality:

Our illuminator, Jesus, [came] down and was crucified. And he bore a crown of thorns. And he put on a purple garment. And he was [crucified] on a tree and he was buried in a tomb. And he rose from the dead.

But Peter continues: "My brothers, Jesus is a stranger to this suffering. But we are the ones who have suffered at the transgression of the mother." Though she is unnamed in this

Nag Hammadi treatise, she is Sophia, who foolishly wanted to procreate without authority from the Father.

One clear exception to the usual Gnostic denial of Jesus' corporality in the Nag Hammadi collection occurs in *Melchizedek*. The writing, a Christianized Sethian Gnostic work, apparently tries to identify Jesus Christ with the mysterious priest figure Melchizedek (mentioned in Gen. 14:18–20; Ps. 110:4; and in the Letter to the Hebrews). One passage refutes claims that "the Savior" was not mortal and therefore did not undergo death and resurrection:

They will say of him that he is unbegotten though he has been begotten, (that) he does not eat even though he eats, (that) he does not drink even though he drinks, (that) he is uncircumcised though he has been circumcised, (that) he is unfleshly though he has been circumcised, (that) he is unfleshly though he has come in flesh, (that) he did not come to suffering ⟨though⟩* he came to suffering, (that) he did not rise from the dead ⟨though⟩ he arose from (the) dead.

The document's stance on the physical character of Jesus and his suffering is "unparalleled" in Gnostic writings, according to Pearson.

Nevertheless, Jesus' execution is openly acknowledged and interpreted positively in four Nag Hammadi texts classified as Valentinian, that is, belonging to the school of the mid-second-century teacher Valentinus. *The Gospel of Truth* says that Jesus was "patient in accepting sufferings . . . since he knows that his death is life for many." Jesus "was nailed to a tree. . . . He draws himself down to death though life eternal clothes him. Having stripped himself of the perishable rags, he puts on imperishability." *The Tripartite Tractate* says the Savior, who let himself be born as an infant in body and soul, took upon himself "the death of those whom he intended to save." *The Interpretation of Knowledge* says he is both the Savior vulnerable to death and suffering and the Word full of divine power. "I became very small so that through my humility I might take you up to the great height whence you had fallen," the Savior said. *The Treatise on the Resurrection*, cast as a "letter" to one Rheginos, says:

---

*For an explanation of the symbol ⟨, see the Appendix.

Now the Son of God, Rheginos, was Son of Man. He embraced them both, possessing the humanity and the divinity, so that on the one hand he might vanquish death through his being Son of God, and that on the other through the Son of Man the restoration to the Pleroma might occur. . . .

The anonymous author quotes Paul approvingly that the Savior "swallowed up death" (1 Cor. 15:55) and that "we suffered with him, and we arose with him, and we went to heaven with him" (Rom. 8:17; Eph. 2:5–6).

Referring to the four Valentinian texts, Elaine Pagels observes, "Not one of these sources denies that Jesus actually suffered and died; all, apparently, assume it. Yet all are concerned to show how, in his incarnation, Christ transcends human nature, so that in his passion and death he prevails over death by divine power."

Both Pagels and Kurt Rudolph have cited the century-old observation of Adolf von Harnack as insightful: "It is not docetism (in the strict sense) which is the characteristic of Gnostic Christology, but the two-nature doctrine; i.e., the distinction between Jesus and Christ, or the doctrine that the redeemer as redeemer did not become man."

Heresy-fighter Irenaeus, who paid special attention to the Valentinians, believed the Gnostic distinction was enough to expel them from the church. Despite the fact that the Valentinians will join other Christians in confessing that the Savior suffered and died, Irenaeus said, they are wolves in sheep's clothing. "Their doctrine is murderous," Irenaeus said.

Pagels acknowledged that the Valentinians' doctrine was different from that of Irenaeus. "But what is so heretical, so dangerous, so blasphemous, about this interpretation of Christian doctrine?" Pagels asked in the Valentinian seminar at the 1978 Yale symposium.

She said that she is convinced the battles over heresy and orthodoxy were fought not only for doctrinal purity, but for social and political reasons. In this case, she said, the defense of Christ's physical suffering was tied to the defense of martyrdom, the willingness to "imitate the passion of Christ." At Lyon, Irenaeus succeeded a bishop who died a martyr, and two anti-Gnostic church leaders of an earlier time, Ignatius and Justin, died in persecution for being Christians, to name only a few examples. Ignatius, circa 100, declared that if, as unbelievers say, Jesus Christ's suffering was only an appearance, "then why am I a prisoner, and why do I long to fight with the wild beasts?"

The Christian Gnostics, in the view of the church fathers, denied the need for martyrdom or lacked enthusiasm for it. Little is found concerning martyrdom in Nag Hammadi texts, except in two writings attributed to James, the brother of Jesus, who was stoned to death around 62 C.E.

The Second Apocalypse of James, a decidedly Christian Gnostic work, gives a graphic account of James being dragged, stomped on, then stoned while standing in a hole he was forced to dig himself. As he is being stoned, James recites a long prayer to "my God and my Father" and confesses his continuing faith.

The Apocryphon of James, considered by many scholars to be minimally Gnostic if at all, has the resurrected Jesus urge his disciples toward martyrdom, to choose suffering and death to become better than himself. "Do you not know that you . . . have yet to be shut up in prison, and condemned unlawfully, and crucified without reason, and buried (shamefully) as (was) I myself?" None who fear death will be saved, he says.

The ways that Christian Gnostic believers dealt with the cross ranged from shocking to subtle—from the laughing Jesus who eludes his ignorant persecutors to a savior who survived in a mystery not much different from orthodox formulations. The range of Gnostic ideas uncovered in Nag Hammadi texts have challenged modern stereotypes of Gnosticism and Docetism. But the greatest challenge to the church occurred in the second century from men who had a way with words.

14. Valentinus, the Formidable Gnostic

Sometime in the middle of the second century, church authorities held an election for a new bishop of Rome, and the loser was a brilliant religious thinker, an Egyptian born and educated man with a Latin name, Valentinus. The man chosen bishop over Valentinus was referred to in sketchy historical accounts as a "martyr"—possibly Pius, who became pope about 143 C.E. Or possibly the winner was Anicetus, whose episcopacy of Rome extended from about 154 to 165 C.E. At any rate, "Valentinus came to Rome in the time of Hyginus, flourished under Pius, and remained until Anicetus," reported Irenaeus.

Valentinus found a school of thought branded by Irenaeus as multiheaded and bewildering. "Every day everyone of them invents something new, and none of them is considered perfect unless he is productive in this way." One of Valentinus's best-known disciples was Ptolemaeus, whose pupil Heracleon wrote the first systematic exegesis, or interpretation, of the Gospel of John.

Churchman Tertullian, of a later generation than Valentinus, said Valentinus and another heretic, Marcion, had been "cast out [of the church] once and again." Historical evidence is lacking about whether Valentinus turned more Gnostic after losing the election, or whether he lost the election because of his Gnostic view of Christianity.

Tertullian had grudging admiration for Valentinus ". . . because both as to talent and eloquence he was an able man." Another church father, Jerome, had a backhand compliment for Valentinus too. "No one can bring a heresy into being unless he is possessed, by nature, of an outstanding intellect and has gifts provided by God. Such a person was Valentinus."

Valentinus and his disciples drew more critical comment from church fathers than did any other Gnostic group. As a result, Christian scholars in later centuries were able to put together a rough idea of Valentinian Gnosticism. The long descriptions by Irenaeus and others of Valentinianism have persuaded scholars that Gnosticism had its primary intellectual flowering in second-century Valentinian writings.

The mythology is summarized nicely by Hans Jonas in *The Gnostic Religion*. In the beginning was the Fore-Father or Abyss, entirely incomprehensible. With him was Silence, also called Grace or Thought. When the Abyss decided to conceive, Silence brought forth Mind, who alone could comprehend the greatness of the Fore-Father.

Mind is also called the Only-Begotten and Father. With him, Truth (a feminine word) was produced, thus forming two original male-female pairs: Abyss (m.) and Silence (f.), Mind (m.) and Truth (f.).

Then Mind, together with his consort, projected the pair Word (m.) and Life (f.). From them was emitted Man (m.) and Church (f.). These eight entities constituted what the Valentinians called the Ogdoad. The last two pairs, wishing to glorify the Father, produced more emanations. This led to the completion of the thirty aeons that make up the Pleroma, literally, the "Fullness" of divine entities.

The last feminine figure in the chain is Sophia, who leapt farthest. She made a passionate attempt to find, or comprehend, the Father, but because it was impossible, she fell into great agony. She was stopped in her quest by a power called Limit. Limit reconciled her to her inability to comprehend the Father, but left behind were her expended passions, a formless entity the Valentinians sometimes called an "abortion."

The other aeons, disturbed by Sophia's sighs over her abortion, appealed to the Father for help. The unknowable one produced a new pair—Christos and the Holy Spirit. Christos brings calm to the aeon hierarchy and also puts form into the abortion, which was necessarily cast out of the Pleroma. That form becomes the so-called lower Sophia, or Achamoth (from the Hebrew word for "wisdom," *hokhmah*).

The lower Sophia is outside the Light and the Pleroma, but she nevertheless seeks it. Alone in the outer darkness she is subjected to every kind of suffering imaginable. "Now she wept and grieved because she was left alone in the Darkness and the Void," according to Irenaeus. But when she thought of the Light "she became cheerful and laughed," only to fall again into fear and bewilderment. Jonas says the lower Sophia "repeats on her own level the scale of emotions which her mother in the Pleroma underwent, the only difference being that these passions now pass over into the form of definitive states of being, and as such they can become the substance of the world."

The mechanics of this creation were made possible by the aeon Jesus, who was formed from the calmed unity of the Pleroma. Christos could not leave the Pleroma, but Jesus was sent both as the consort of the lower Sophia and as her savior, that is, one who would free her from her passions.

The lower Sophia's pleas resulted in the creation of the Creator God (called the Demiurge in Valentinianism) and everything pertaining to human souls. From the rest of the lower Sophia's passions came the basic materials of the cosmos: from her tears, the water; from her laughter, the luminaries (sun and stars); from her grief and shock, the more solid elements of the world. (Laughter in this Gnostic system is associated with happy thoughts of light!)

Three human elements were derived from the experiences of the lower Sophia, and they are important in understanding the salvation message of the Valentinian Gnostics. The human body was the result of her passions, the soul came from her pleas, and the spirit from the reception of light from her savior. Humans, aware of their bodies and souls but not of the divine light or spirit in themselves, finally are rescued after the aeon Jesus descends on the human Jesus at his baptism in the Jordan River. This divinely infilled Jesus then spreads the gnosis to humankind. The spirits in humans, saved by this knowledge, are ultimately destined to enter the Pleroma with their "Mother," the lower Sophia.

"According to Gnostic ideas," says Jan Zandee of the Netherlands, "sin is ignorance and salvation is the imparting of true knowledge concerning God. But the basis of ignorance lies in God himself, since by virtue of his nature He is unknowable." The supreme God, in other words, emanates aspects of himself that are deficient (except for the only-begotten Mind) in that they don't know the Father. "The further from the source of light, the blacker is the darkness of ignorance in which the creature lives," says Zandee.

There is a philosophical need to distinguish between the unity of the Pleroma and the inadequacies of the world, and it can be seen also in texts of the Valentinian school in the Nag Hammadi library. "The aeons (of the Pleroma) were not cut off from the Father, but he spreads out over them," says *The Tripartite Tractate*. "Strong is the system of the Pleroma; small is that which broke loose (and) became the world," says *The Treatise on the Resurrection*.

Irenaeus said Valentinians disagreed with one another, and differences have been noted in the celestial systems in Nag Hammadi's collection of Valentinian works. Beside the aforementioned *Tripartite Tractate, Treatise on the Resurrection, Interpretation of Knowledge*, and *Gospel of Truth*, the library contains a *Valentinian Exposition*, which includes ritual pronouncements for anointing, baptism, and Eucharist. *The Gospel of Philip*, a collage of cryptic aphorisms and comments, includes some material from Valentinian thought.

Most attention has focused on *The Gospel of Truth* because of its striking quality and the possibility that Valentinus himself was the author. Irenaeus said the Valentinian church read a "Gospel of Truth," but it is not possible to know if this is it. In form, it resembles a sermon. It does not provide a continuous narration of Jesus' life, death, and resurrection as found in the New Testament gospels. The term "gospel" in the opening line of the work preserves the term's meaning of "good news," as it was so often used by Paul. The writing begins:

The gospel of truth is joy for those who have received from the Father of truth the grace of knowing him, through the power of the Word that came forth from the pleroma, the one who is in the thought and the mind of the Father, that is, the one who is addressed as the Savior, (that) being the name of the work he is to perform for the redemption of those who were ignorant of the Father, while the name [of] the gospel is the proclamation of hope, being discovery for those who search for him.

Among the earliest scholars favoring Valentinus as author of

Nag Hammadi's *Gospel of Truth* were W. C. van Unnik, Kendrick Grobel, Robert M. Grant, and Benoit Standaert.

To take that position, scholars must concede that the text has no detailed list of aeons, no split between Christ and Jesus, and no mention of a Demiurge, that is, no distinction between a higher and a lower God. Most striking is the absence of Sophia, although some scholars believe that her role is taken by "error."

Error appears early in *The Gospel of Truth* in passages that seem to hark back to Sophia's anguish and her attempts to comprehend the Father:

Ignorance of the Father brought about anguish and terror; and the anguish grew solid like a fog, so that no one was able to see. For this reason, error became powerful; it worked on its own matter foolishly, not having known the truth.

MacRae says that "because this account is of itself not readily intelligible without a knowledge of the Sophia myth, one may conclude that *The Gospel of Truth* is a later formulation which presupposes the earlier, perhaps less sophisticated, myth."

Bentley Layton, in *The Gnostic Scriptures*, says that "error" combines both Sophia and Ialdabaoth from the Gnostic myth. That is a virtual necessity because of the twofold role that "error" plays in *The Gospel of Truth*. Error resembles Sophia when the evolution of the cosmos is described, but *The Gospel of Truth* also says that error persecuted Jesus—something Sophia/Wisdom never does in Gnostic writings. That is the role of the evil Archon.

Layton says the eloquence of *The Gospel of Truth* plus comparisons with fragments of Valentinus's writing quoted by church fathers makes it "extremely likely" that Valentinus composed the sermon. "One of the most brilliantly crafted works of ancient Christian literature, the original Greek it must have had a rhetorical power that ranked with the great masterpieces of Christian prose," Layton writes.

Today's readers, however, should not be surprised if they find the writing to be confusing. It isn't simply due to the fact that it is an English translation of a Coptic translation of the original Greek. Harold W. Attridge of Notre Dame has concluded that the work deliberately "conceals major elements of the system which it presupposes." The aim, Attridge says, was to "make an appeal to ordinary Christians, inviting them to share the basic insights of Valentinianism." But in doing so, the author of the text gives familiar New Testament ideas and language new and unfamiliar meanings.

"Similarly elusive is the frame of reference of the text, which seems to slip quite easily from cosmic to historical, then to personal or psychological perspectives," writes Attridge in a new introduction for the work in the revised edition of *The Nag Hammadi Library in English.*

As for whether Valentinus authored it, Attridge concludes, "That remains a distinct possibility, although it cannot be definitively established." Whatever its precise date and authorship, Attridge says it was a work "by a consummate literary artist."

Some passages would have been a credit to the most orthodox of Christian preachers. Speaking of Jesus, the author says:

When light had spoken through his mouth, as well as his voice which gave birth to life, he gave them thought and understanding and mercy and salvation and the powerful spirit from the infiniteness and the sweetness of the Father. . . . He became a way for those who were gone astray and knowledge for those who were ignorant, a discovery for those who were searching and a support for those who were wavering, immaculateness for those who were defiled.

A charitable concern might be read into the following:

Make firm the foot of those who have stumbled and stretch out your hands to those who are ill. Feed those who are hungry and give repose to those who are weary, and raise up those who wish to rise, and awaken those who sleep.

It could also be understood figuratively, in that knowledge should be fed to those who "hunger" for the truth. Awakening the ignorant from their "sleep" or "dream" is a metaphor also used elsewhere in *The Gospel of Truth.*

The savior's task, the author says, is to inform people that they have "places" of "rest" in the highest realm. Jesus "has brought many back from error. He has gone before them to their places from which they had moved away."

Therefore, if one has knowledge, he is from above. If he is called, he hears, he answers, and he turns to him who is calling him, and ascends to him. and he knows in what manner he is called. Having knowledge, he does the will of the one who called him, he wishes to be pleasing to him, he receives rest.

The idea of "ascending" to one's heavenly place was apparently conveyed through rituals in the Valentinian churches, but *The Gospel of Truth* does not overtly refer to rituals.

The author, whoever he was, must have been "a well-read and gifted theologian with a deep sense of true piety," writes Helmut Koester in his *Introduction to the New Testament*, volume 2. "Although there are no explicit quotations in the writing, the author not only knew the Old Testament very well, but also the gospels of the New Testament and the letters of Paul," Koester says in his 1982 textbook.

Despite the inability to prove Valentinus was the author, Koester advises that "no one should miss the opportunity of reading this book, or be deterred by either its possibly late date or its authorship by one of the archheretics of the Christian church. Its study is rewarding—especially after the laborious study of the documents of mythological Gnosticism."

15. Feminine Imagery: Rites and Roles

Considered one of the worst heresies experienced by Christianity for eighteen hundred years, Gnosticism has borne long after its demise the stigma of a religious philosophy that sometimes induced believers into lives of debauchery. Some Gnostic sects, their church opponents said, engaged in rituals that were more sexual than sacred.

If there were Gnostic writings that justified libertine attitudes, however, they were not in the Nag Hammadi collection. No sanction for amoral behavior seems to be explicitly or implicitly stated. No text has been identified, for example, with the philosophy of Simon Magus and his alleged whore-companion Helena, or with any priests who concocted love potions.

Some texts, in fact, indicate that ascetic withdrawal is the most desirable response to the lusts of the world. "Woe to you who love intimacy with womankind and polluted intercourse with them!" Jesus is made to say in *The Book of Thomas the Contender*. The Nag Hammadi library may not be representative of the full range of Gnostic literature. Its collectors were most likely people associated at one time or another with the monastic system founded by Pachomius, perhaps monks at the basilica near the cliffs of Jabal al-Tarif.

Between descriptions by orthodox fathers of Gnostics defiling women and the possibility that ascetic men collected the Nag Hammadi texts, the chances would seem slim that a respectable view of women would emerge from Gnostic literature. Yet one striking element in the Jewish Gnostic and Christian Gnostic writings is the prominent role played by feminine figures. Scholars, especially feminists, have searched for clues that Gnostics may have had a relatively favorable outlook toward the feminine in spiritual matters. Moreover, some women scholars are hopeful that Gnostic literature from Nag Hammadi may demonstrate that the Judeo-Christian heritage was not devoid of powerful female symbols of the divine. Well-educated Christian women today face strong challenges from their peers, who say their tradition of belief is hopelessly dominated by masculine imagery.

There is always a need for caution about whether the sources—the church fathers or the new texts—really tell enough to form judgments on Gnostic outlooks: the bishops of old were not free of bias and the Gnostic texts deal more with the metaphysical than with the mundane. Nonetheless, references to religious rites in those two resources may help. They suggest that women played active parts, although some church fathers claimed it was limited to being duped.

Irenaeus said women were especially attracted to heretical groups. Even in his own Rhone Valley, where he was bishop, he said the Gnostic teacher Marcus had attracted "many foolish women," including the wife of one of Irenaeus's deacons. The church father said Marcus was a self-proclaimed prophet and magician who would pray over a cup of purple liquid mixed with wine, a concoction Marcus said was the blood of Grace, the aeon also known as Silence in the Valentinian Pleroma.

Marcus would have a woman taste of the cup and allow Grace to flow into her. "He concerns himself in particular with women, especially with those of high rank, the elegantly attired and wealthy, whom he frequently attempts to lead astray by flattering them and saying, 'I desire to make thee a partaker of my Grace.' "

Marcus suggested that the way to do that was to come together, said Irenaeus. " 'Adorn thyself as a bride who expects her bridegroom, that thou mayest be what I am, and I what thou art. Receive in thy bridechamber the seed of light. Receive from me the bridegroom, and give him a place, and have a place in him. Behold, Grace has descended upon thee; open thy mouth and prophesy.' "

If the woman replies, "I have never prophesied before, nor can I prophesy," then Marcus offers some more prayers and exhorts her to try again. The woman, "deluded and puffed up by what has been said," according to Irenaeus, takes the risk and heart pounding, she utters "ridiculous nonsense," anything that comes into her head. Convinced by Marcus that she is a prophetess, she thanks him profusely for sharing Grace with her.

"She tries to repay him, not only with a gift of her possessions—by which he has collected a great deal of money—but also by physical intercourse, prepared as she is to be united with him in everything in order that she, with him, may enter into the One." Irenaeus indicated he knew of Marcus's antics from the women who had returned to "the church of God" and confessed that they had loved Marcus with violent passion. The disciples of Marcus were said to have similarly deceived many women. "They claim they are in the heights beyond every power," Irenaeus said, "and as a result are free to do anything."

The story of Marcus and his lustful disciples, of course, is not from the Nag Hammadi library but from the polemics of Irenaeus. Still, some Gnostics did have a bridal chamber ceremony. The Pleroma seemed to be the setting for the Valentinian bridal chamber described by church fathers. It is a future celestial scene in which marriages are to be performed between Sophia and Jesus and between the human spirits and the bridegrooms, the angels. When the restoration of the Pleroma is complete, the world will then be extinguished in the fire of ignorance.

In the Nag Hammadi library, *The Exegesis on the Soul* tells of the wanderings of the female half of the soul who goes from one adultery to another. She appeals to heaven, is purified through baptism, and is reunited with her male partner in a bridal chamber, and they become one in a lustless way.

The bridal chamber is mentioned prominently in Nag Hammadi's *The Gospel of Philip*. Like other Gnostic "gospels," it is not the story of Jesus' life, but a series of commentaries. *Philip* may have been written about the second half of the second century in the area of Antioch, says German scholar Martin Krause.

Jesus emerges as a mystery-laden figure in *Philip*, whose author "reveals" the relative importance of the names Jesus, Christ, and Nazarene. Jesus himself appeared in different forms to different people—to the great as great, to the small as small, said *Philip*. In fact, the Lord did "everything in a mystery, a baptism and a chrism [anointing] and a eucharist and a redemption and a bridal chamber."

The mystery of worldly marriage is such that no one but the

man and wife know the day when they have intercourse, *Philip*
declares. But if this marriage of "defilement" is hidden, "how
much more is the undefiled marriage a true mystery. It is not
fleshy but pure. It does not belong to desire, but to the will. It
does not belong to the darkness or the night, but it belongs to
the day and the light."

The ritual in *Philip* apparently involves the symbolic marriage
of one's spirit to its heavenly counterpart. It is a means of salvation, for *Philip* says if one becomes "a child of the bridal chamber" one receives the light. If one does not receive the sacrament
on earth, one will not receive the light in the world to come.

The bridal chamber "is the supreme secret" for the author of
The Gospel of Philip, according to Jorunn Jacobsen Buckley. "Only
by acquiring male or female power, respectively, may the female
or male human being delude the evil powers," she says. "The
full-fledged Gnostic in *The Gospel of Philip* transforms himself
into a unified, resurrected being in the bridal chamber."

Philip gives the theory behind the ceremony without describing
the rite itself—except to say it was not lustful. An indelicate rite
of the Phibionites, a Gnostic sect in Alexandria, was recounted
by Epiphanius, a church father who seemed to have some personal knowledge of the group. After an orgy, the members offered up menstrual blood and semen in a rite patterned after
the Christian Eucharist, Epiphanius wrote.

Bringing more children into the world only furthered the purpose of the archons, but the Phibionite practice short-circuited
that process and, in the sect's view, constituted a sacrifice to the
divine. "The incorporation of the mensus as the blood of Christ
alongside the body of Christ in the Phibionite ritual underscores
the positive involvement of the woman. She, too, contains a part
of the divine which must and can be gathered," says James E.
Goehring, former associate director of the Institute for Antiquity
and Christianity in Claremont. A late Gnostic writing, *Pistis Sophia*, curses in the name of Jesus the people "who take male
semen and female menstrual blood and make it into a lentil dish
and eat it."

The alleged Phibionite practice is not likely to be cited frequently as a positive example of the equality of women in spir-

itual life. But quotable today in the light of the increasing numbers of women ministers and priests are the fuming remarks of another church father, Tertullian, around 200 C.E.: "These heretical women—how audacious they are! They have no modesty; they are bold enough to teach, to engage in argument, to enact exorcisms, to undertake cures, and, it may be, even to baptize!"

Irenaeus said the woman Gnostic teacher Marcellina appeared in Rome in the mid-second century representing the Carpocratian Gnostic group from Alexandria. The Carpocratians claimed to have received secret teachings from Mary, Salome, and Martha—women mentioned in New Testament Gospels.

Other than the Gospel of Mark, which disparages certain women followers and the mother of Jesus, the New Testament gospels depict women with positive roles in Jesus' life. A hint of spiritual equality for women in very early Christianity was reflected in a formula recited by Paul to the Galatians (3:28) that after baptism there is no distinction between male and female. Paul himself did not seem to share the same enthusiasm.

Texts used by Gnostic Christians would seem to reflect that early strain of the Jesus movement that honored women. In the Berlin Museum's *Gospel of Mary*, Peter says to Mary: "Sister, we know that the Savior loved you more than the rest of the women. Tell us the words of the Savior which you remember."

Mary relates what the Savior told her and concludes with a story of how the soul safely passes by seven powers of wrath on its heavenly ascent.

When she finishes, Andrew questions whether the Savior really said that. "For certainly these teachings are strange ideas," Andrew says.

"Did he really speak with a woman without our knowledge (and) not openly?" Peter asks.

Breaking into tears, Mary responds: "My brother, Peter, what do you think? Do you think that I thought this up myself in my heart, or that I am lying about the Savior?"

Levi comes to Mary's defense. "Peter, you have always been hot-tempered. Now I see you contending against the woman like the adversaries. But if the Savior made her worthy, who are you indeed to reject her? Surely the Savior knows her very well. That is why he loved her more than us." Levi urges the disciples to "put on the perfect man," disperse and preach the gospel, which, according to *The Gospel of Mary*, they did.

A similar exchange between Peter and Mary occurs in *Pistis Sophia*, but Jesus supports Mary. The inspiration for the story in *Pistis Sophia* easily could have been *The Gospel of Mary* and/or *The Gospel of Thomas*, the last saying of which (114) conveys the same sense of the worthiness of Mary over a carping Peter:

Simon Peter said to them, "Let Mary leave us, for women are not worthy of life."

Jesus said, "I myself shall lead her in order to make her male, so that she too may become a living spirit resembling you males. For every woman who will make herself male will enter the kingdom of heaven."

Jesus defends Mary in the face of Peter's criticism—she too will become a living spirit and enter the kingdom. But the statement is otherwise dismaying to scholars pleased by the prominence of women in Gnostic tradition. (*Thomas* 114 is often considered now to be a Gnostic addition to the collection of Jesus sayings.)

The seemingly antifeminine tone of 114 is mitigated somewhat by the widespread Hellenistic idea that perfection is obtained philosophically by uniting femaleness with maleness. The Jewish philosopher Philo of Alexandria wrote: "Progress is indeed nothing else than the giving up of the female gender by changing into the male, since the female gender is material, passive, corporeal, and sense-perceptible, while the male is active, rational, incorporeal and more akin to mind and thought." *The First Apocalypse of James* from Nag Hammadi says the female element (perishability) has attained to the male element (imperishability). A sermon in *Zostrianos* urges, "Flee from the madness and bondage of femaleness, and choose for yourself the salvation of maleness." The Naassene Gnostics were said by Hippolytus to believe that "when men come (to the gate of heaven) they must lay down their clothing and all become bridegrooms, being rendered wholly male through the virgin spirit." This Naassene statement suggests bridal chamber imagery, but it is impossible to know in such cases if an actual ceremony was involved.

Mary is the most commonly employed woman disciple in these

apocryphal dialogues, but Salome makes a brief appearance in another exchange in *The Gospel of Thomas*. Mark describes Salome as one of the women who had followed Jesus in Galilee and ministered to him, then had witnessed his crucifixion and later went to the tomb (Mark 15:40–41; 16:1). (Salome also appears as a skeptical foil in the apocryphal *Protoevangelium of James*.)

In *Thomas* 61, Salome asks Jesus, "Who are you, man, that you have come up on my couch and eaten from my table?" Dinner guests in Mediterranean antiquity normally reclined on couches placed near the table.

Jesus replies, "I am he who exists from the undivided. I was given of the things of my father." Salome says, "I am your disciple." Jesus says, "Therefore I say, if he is destroyed, he will be filled with light, but if he is divided, he will be filled with darkness." The obscure nature of Jesus' responses aside, the exchange is significant because Salome is depicted as claiming to be his disciple.

In Nag Hammadi's *Dialogue of the Savior*, Mary has an equal role with Matthew and Judas in questioning Jesus, who is primarily called "the Lord" here. No identification is given for Mary or Judas. The opening line of the text indicates Jesus is addressing his disciples. (There is no suggestion here that Judas Iscariot was meant. This document probably counted Judas, the brother of Jesus, as a disciple. The significance of this will be discussed later.)

The Dialogue of the Savior praises Mary: "She spoke as a woman who understood completely." At the same time, the Lord tells the three to "pray in the place where there is no woman" and to "destroy the works of womanhood." From the context of this discussion it appears that the works of femaleness refer to having children—an act that perpetuates one's attachment to earthly burdens.

The Gospel of Philip, which often reinterprets New Testament tradition, says the companion of the Savior is Mary Magdalene. He loved her "more than [all] the disciples [and used to] kiss her [often] on her [. . .]." The rest of the disciples asked why, and the author has Jesus give an oblique answer implying that the disciples are blind.

The claim in *Philip* that Jesus kissed Mary does not necessarily suggest erotic intentions. At another point *Philip* says that "we kiss one another" because "we receive conception from the grace which is in one another"—apparently a step to "become perfect" spiritually. Granted, the kiss is loaded with more meaning in *Philip* than in some other sources. Jesus greets his brother James with a kiss on the mouth in *The Second Apocalypse of James*. The "holy kiss" exchanged between Christians is documented even in the New Testament (Acts 20:37; Rom. 16:16; 1 Cor. 16:20; 2 Cor. 13:12; 1 Thess. 5:26; and 1 Pet. 5:14).

Whatever unusual respect for women believers might have existed in the beginnings of the Jesus movement was undercut in the churches of the late first century and during the second century, according to Elaine Pagels. Her popular 1979 book *The Gnostic Gospels* proposes that Christian orthodoxy developed much of its doctrine and church structure in reaction to Gnostic ideas and practices. Pagels's most influential contribution may have been in pointing out the Gnostic openness to the feminine and the contrasting attitudes of the church hierarchy.

Pagels says the "antifeminist element in Paul's views" was exaggerated in later Letters composed as if Paul had written them. In 1 Timothy, one of several pseudo-Pauline Letters in the New Testament, "Paul" says (2:11–15):

Let a woman learn in silence with all submissiveness. I permit no woman to teach or to have authority over men; she is to keep silent. For Adam was formed first, then Eve; and Adam was not deceived, but the woman was deceived and became a transgressor. Yet woman will be saved through bearing children, if she continues in faith and love and holiness, with modesty.

As seen in those passages, one's understanding of the Genesis story affected how women were to be perceived. The very different Gnostic reading of Genesis—in which Eve is a hero—may have contributed to their favorable view.

"In 1 and 2 Timothy, Colossians and Ephesians, 'Paul' insists that women be subordinate to men," Pagels says. "The letter of Titus, in Paul's name, directs the selection of bishops in terms that entirely exclude women from consideration. Literally and figuratively, the bishop is to be a father figure to the congregation."

Before 200 c.e., *The Apostolic Church Order* appeared in orthodox churches. In this document, cited by Pagels, the apostles are
depicted discussing controversial questions. With Mary and Martha present, John says:

When the Master blessed the bread and the cup and signed them with
the words, "This is my body and blood," he did not offer it to the
women who are with us. Martha said, "He did not offer it to Mary,
because he saw her laugh." Mary said, "I no longer laugh; he said to
us before, as he taught, 'Your weakness is redeemed through
strength.' "

Mary's argument fails, and Pagels says the document adds that
the male disciples agree for this reason that no woman shall become a priest. Pagels ends her comment on *The Apostolic Church
Order* there, but more could be said about the orthodox writing
in terms of Christian Gnostic belief and ritual.

Mary's offense was that she laughed! Laughter, it is true, can
be a sign of mockery or silliness—often considered inappropriate for church settings. New Testament writings condone joy
and rejoicing but rarely speak of laughing. But the Nag Hammadi corpus does. And an early reconstruction of a text includes
laughter from Mary!

In *The Dialogue of the Savior*, as translated in the 1977 edition
of *The Nag Hammadi Library in English*, Mary asks, "O Lord, behold, when I am bearing the body, [for what reason do I] weep,
and for what reason do I [laugh]?" The Lord answers, "[If you]
weep because of its deeds [you will] abide, and the mind laughs
[. . .] spirit." Despite the fragmentary state of the text, it seems
that weeping is associated with lament over bodily existence and
laughing is linked to thoughts of spiritual things.

That is a consistent Gnostic viewpoint. It is found also in *The
Gospel of Philip*, where it is claimed that the Lord said "some have
entered the kingdom of heaven laughing." For the second edition of *The Nag Hammadi Library in English* translators tended to
attempt fewer reconstructions of missing words. The first-edi-
tion translation of *Philip*, with conjectured words between brack-
ets, offers an explanation for why some would enter the kingdom laughing:

As soon as [Christ went down into] the water he came [out laughing at] everything (of this world), [not] because [he considers it] a trifle, but [because he is full of] contempt for it. He who [wants to enter] the kingdom of [heaven will attain it]. If he despises [everything (of this world)] and scorns it as a trifle, [he will come] out laughing. So it is also with the bread and cup and the oil, even though there is another one superior to these.

Philip thus connects laughing with the sacraments, including the bread and cup of the Eucharist—a connection that was also made in *The Apostolic Church Order*.

Dare it be suggested that some Christian Gnostics included laughter in their ceremonies for baptism, Eucharist, and anointing in a kind of imitation of Christ's scorn of worldly powers? Rituals have the potential of reminding the faithful of their spiritual triumph over the world, as told in sacred stories. The Savior laughed at his would-be crucifiers in Christian Gnostic lore, just as Eve-Sophia laughed at the would-be rapists in the Garden. Mary seems to weep over her mortal state but laughs when her mind thinks of the spiritual world in *The Dialogue of the Savior*. A parallel exists in Irenaeus's report that Valentinians believed that Sophia wept when she was alone in the darkness and void but she became cheerful and laughed when she thought of the Light.

The Christian Gnostic treatment of Mary as a disciple, indeed a favorite of Jesus, could have been disputed by the orthodox church on the basis of the New Testament. But *The Apostolic Church Order* denigrates Mary to a point unjustified by Scripture. It may thus betray a polemic against Mary as an authority in Christian Gnostic circles. The orthodox text restored Mary as an acceptable figure in church lore by having her repentantly end her laughing. But it is also made clear that women cannot be spiritual peers of men—perhaps in contrast to Gnostic practice.

The number of women scholars interested in Gnostic studies has multiplied since Pagels broached her theories. Not all are sure the research is promising, but Karen King of Occidental College is more sanguine, saying it recovers previously unknown church history and recaptures images of powerful female deities. Even if heretical, the Gnostic heroines are still part of the Judeo-Christian heritage—as opposed to pagan goddesses and Eastern deities that an influential minority of feminists have looked to for new models of spirituality.

King was the principal organizer in 1985 of a conference on "Images of the Feminine in Gnosticism" in Claremont and Anaheim. "The conference proved to be both heady with excitement and deflating to me," said Elizabeth Clark of Duke University, who was asked to sum up the twenty-one conference papers and discussions. Despite all the female figures in the texts, Clark said her impression was that evidence was meager to say women were equals in Gnosticism.

King acknowledged that, as in *The Apocryphon of John*, the female is often secondary to the male. "Deficiency is caused by the female working alone. Salvation comes when male and female work in concert, though always with the male/father in a position more primary than that of the female/mother, both in terms of sequence and in terms of power." On the positive side for feminist concerns, King said, the female figures in this and other works are never depicted as passive or weak.

The publication of *The Nag Hammadi Library in English* in 1977 and of Pagels's book two years later prompted unfavorable assessments from conservative commentators on the worth of the manuscript find as a whole. Dale Vree, reviewing both books for the *National Catholic Register*, said that contrary to the sympathetic treatment by Robinson the texts "are just plain silly" when read from the perspective of faith. "The gnostic writings as a whole lack coherence. . . . Indeed, it was part of the gnostic mystique to be 'spiritually creative.'" Pagels's book, Vree contended, would only harm the "push for priestesses" today because it would be seen as a project of the heretical Gnostics. "Thus, I don't really think the publication of the Nag Hammadi manuscripts poses any serious threat to the Faith today (though they were undoubtedly a mortal threat in the days of the early Church)."

Pagels ended her book with a disclaimer that as a historian she did not advocate "going back" to Gnosticism, much less that she sided with it against orthodox Christianity. She later said in an interview that she wished she had put the disclaimer at the front of her book.

Expanding on that point in a 1982 lecture, she said, "I do not mean to say that church leaders acted in a deliberately Machiavellian way to suppress gnostic Christianity, simply to consolidate their own power and importance." She pointed out that sociologist Max Weber has shown that the religious movements that survive are those that develop effective institutions within the first several generations of the founder's death. "Had the Christian movement not developed such institutional structures, it probably would have disappeared among hundreds of other Greco-Roman cults," she said. "I believe that we owe the survival of Christian tradition to the organizational and theological structure that the orthodox church developed. But the discovery at Nag Hammadi allows us to see, for the first time, what was lost in the process—some remarkable alternate views of Jesus and his message," Pagels said.

A similar rationale for appreciating the Nag Hammadi find was given by Layton. "After the official Christianization of the late Roman Empire (A.D. 313–381), theological objections to the gnostic scriptures were given the force of law, and most copies of these scriptures were banned and eventually perished," he writes. "Orthodox Christian doctrine of the ancient world—and thus of modern church—was partly conceived of as being what gnostic scripture was *not*," Layton continues. "For this reason, a knowledge of gnostic scripture is indispensable for anyone who hopes to understand the historical roots of Christian theology and belief."

The strongest criticism of Pagels's book and Nag Hammadi studies in general was issued in 1980 by Jesuit biblical scholar Joseph A. Fitzmyer, professor of New Testament at Catholic University of America. In a review of *The Gnostic Gospels* for *America* magazine, Fitzmyer referred to "gnostic Pagels" and to "gibberish" and "schlock that is supposed to pass for 'literature' in the Nag Hammadi library."

Part of Fitzmyer's displeasure derived from his contention that Christian Gnostics "were simply not around" for the first century of Christian existence, only "Christians with protognostic tendencies at the end of the first century." That question has had many good scholars on opposite sides, and Fitzmyer mused: "It has been mystifying, indeed, why serious scholars continue to talk about the pertinence of this material to the study of the New Testament."

Fitzmyer may be right in thinking that it is difficult to prove a direct influence of the classic Gnostic myth on the New Testament, although the proposed Gnostic influence on the prologue of the Gospel of John may be an exception. What seems undeniably important for New Testament studies, however, is that some Nag Hammadi texts, despite Gnostic additions, have preserved valuable words and ideas from the early Jesus movement. In this research, the focus is not on Gnostic elements in the texts. The attention is on authentic traditions about Jesus transmitted independently of the New Testament and recaptured for modern critical study.

IV. THE JESUS OF HISTORY

16. The Apocryphal Jesus and Respectability

"I won't say the papers misquote me," said Senator Barry Goldwater at one point in his unsuccessful 1964 campaign for the U.S. presidency, "but I sometimes wonder where Christianity would be today if some of those reporters had been Matthew, Mark, Luke, and John." Columnist Walter Lippmann's response a few days later was that "the senator might remember that the evangelists had a more inspiring subject."

That exchange is pertinent here not so much for what it says about journalism as for illustrating a common misconception about the Christian Gospels. The so-called synoptic Gospels of Matthew, Mark, and Luke are written to a great extent in a matter-of-fact reporting style, complete with quoted dialogue between the principal figures. Yet they are not journalistic reports. The earliest of the Gospels, Mark, was probably written about forty years after Jesus' death. Matthew and Luke borrowed much from Mark and added material they obtained from other sources. By their selection, arrangement, and omissions, the authors of Mark, Matthew, and Luke emphasized what each felt to be important to say about the life and death of Jesus.

The author of the Gospel of John, written around the last decade of the first century, was less interested in a biographical-like treatment. The last of the Gospels, John is mostly concerned with the divine nature of Jesus and contains long discourses and self-descriptions by Jesus.

There is general agreement along these lines in New Testament scholarship. The differences begin over how much credence can be placed on these accounts of Jesus. Conservative Christian scholars tend to accept the Gospels, the whole Bible, in fact, as error free or at least basically accurate and factual. Liberal scholars tend to reject the historicity of parts that seem legendary or mythical—such as the narratives about Jesus' birth, many of the miraculous episodes, and often the "empty tomb" stories, which imply that the resurrection involved the bodily re-suscitation of Jesus. The gradations and varieties of biblical in-terpretation are not all covered by those two characterizations, of course.

More definitive than "conservative" and "liberal" is the divi-sion between those who use historical-critical methods of biblical analysis and those who don't. Those who don't are nearly all conservative Christians who tend to work professionally and/or personally under the constraints of creed or doctrine. Historical-critical scholarship reveals disharmony in early Christianity and its possible branches of development. The predominant ten-dency outside historical-critical circles is to "harmonize" differ-ences seen in the New Testament and to assume that most every-thing said about Jesus and by Jesus was known from the very beginning—and most of all that no New Testament writer would have "invented" words and events. Historical-critical studies demonstrate that the biblical writers did take liberties or trans-mitted theological creative traditions known to them. In this, they were following the accepted literary and religious conven-tions of their era, historians say.

Scholarly attempts to get behind the theology of John and Paul and the narratives and presuppositions of Mark, Matthew, and Luke are called quests for the "historical Jesus." Even these New Testament specialists are aware of limitations, however. As James Robinson points out, the "historical Jesus" is more accurately the "historian's Jesus"—a picture of him and his life reasonably es-tablished by historical-critical means.

In this regard scholars have made "considerable progress to-ward understanding the fantastically creative religious era of which Jesus was a part," says Catholic author-sociologist Andrew M. Greeley, referring to Judaism in the first centuries B.C.E. and C.E. The research involves little "debunking," he says. "New Tes-tament criticism and New Testament history once may have had a strong flavor of agnostic rationalism about them, and even now each new 'discovery' as reported briefly in the daily papers may be taken by some traditional believers as an attack on their faith. In fact, however, most of the scholars are simply interested in understanding better Jesus and his time."

The search for the historical Jesus includes a comparison of Christian works with other literature from the first centuries. Stories about Jesus and transmission of his sayings were probably by word of mouth in the early years after his crucifixion. But between the time of predominantly oral transmission and the New Testament Gospels, "it is beyond doubt" that some written sources existed, declares Helmut Koester of Harvard Divinity School.

A collection of parables in the fourth chapter of Mark and the miracle stories in John are thought to have been derived from written sources. Well established today is the opinion that Matthew and Luke both used Mark and a further written source, the so-called saying source Q, Koester says.

When *The Gospel of Thomas* was discovered among the Nag Hammadi manuscripts, scholars found the closest work yet to Q. *Thomas* is a rather primitive literary piece designed to preserve the words of Jesus, a revealer of ordinary and divine wisdom. There is no connecting narrative, no life story, no crucifixion or resurrection scenes. It strings together about 114 sayings in seemingly random order.

Koester, and other scholars before him, have said that when the New Testament Gospels were written the main purpose was to present the significance of this man-God who suffered, was crucified, and rose again. The traditions about Jesus' words and deeds were incorporated by the Gospel writers, not because of an urge to record his human ministry for history, "but because they serve as parts of a theological introduction to the proclamation of Jesus' passion and death," says Koester. By contrast, someone set down the sayings in *The Gospel of Thomas* for their intrinsic worth rather than as complements to another story.

Despite *The Gospel of Thomas*'s potential for New Testament research, this new sayings source met some resistance even in historical-critical circles because it was not a document that was accepted by the church into the biblical canon, that is, as an authoritative book. The word "apocryphal," for so many scholars, has been synonymous with the word "unacceptable," if not heretical.

Not only that, some critical scholars had been lulled into indifference by the banality of existing apocryphal works. Certain apocryphal books had been preserved by the church because they were innocuous stories expanding on Gospel accounts. A *Gospel of Thomas* already existed, a work pretending to depict the childhood exploits of Jesus. *The Acts of Thomas* is one of many apocryphal acts of the apostles, telling in this case stories of Judas Thomas on a missionary trip to India. *The Protoevangelium of James*, among other things, establishes Mary the mother of Jesus as a perpetual virgin. In this book, a skeptical Salome plays the "doubting Thomas" by saying she must touch the Virgin Mary to be convinced of her continuing virginity right after the birth of Jesus. When Salome does, her hand is burned, but she is miraculously cured after she proclaims her belief and touches the baby Jesus.

The Nag Hammadi library contains two hitherto unknown works of this type: *The Acts of Peter and the Twelve Apostles*, in which Peter and the Twelve meet the risen Christ disguised as a pearl merchant, and *The Apocalypse of Paul*, in which Paul encounters a child (probably the risen Christ) who summons him to some heavenly visions. In 2 Corinthians 12:2–4, Paul describes his mystical ascent to the third heaven; *The Apocalypse of Paul* expands on that by describing his visit from the fourth through the tenth heavens! For various reasons, most of these writings can be dated well into the second century or later and are useful for the illustrating the pious imagination of the church in that time frame.

But from writings of the church fathers it was also known that some early apocryphal "gospels" paid attention to the words of Jesus. Clement of Alexandria said *The Gospel of the Egyptians* has Salome asking the Lord about what would be known. The Lord answers, "When you have trampled on the garment of shame and when the two become one and the male with the female (is) neither male nor female." The idea of the two becoming one— an androgynous being—is similarly stated in *Thomas* 22 (see also *Thomas* 106) and in the mid-second-century sermon called *2 Clement*. Trampling on one's garments is found in *Thomas* 37, a saying that University of Chicago scholar Jonathan Z. Smith says reveals elements of an archaic Christian baptism.

Clement of Alexandria also knew a *Gospel of the Hebrews*. It has a saying very close to no. 2 in *The Gospel of Thomas*: "He that seeks will not rest until he finds; and he that has found shall marvel; and he that has marveled shall reign; and he that has reigned shall rest." Actually, it is closer to *Thomas* 2 in the Greek fragment Papyrus Oxyrhynchus 654, which also concludes with reigning and resting. Variations on the theme of ask, seek, find, or knock appear elsewhere in the Jesus sayings traditions, notably in Q (Matt. 7:7–8; Luke 11:9–10).

Noncanonical writings as the possible carriers of Jesus sayings were not so easily ignorable once the full text of *The Gospel of Thomas* appeared on the scene along with two rudimentary dialogues of disciples with Jesus—*The Dialogue of the Savior* and *The Apocryphon (Secret Book) of James*. The latter two texts have some interesting similarities to each other and to *The Gospel of Thomas*.

Savior and *James* are worth examining first because they represent a step prior to the literary development of the narrative Gospels in the New Testament. The question-and-answer format was seen as a way to weave together individual sayings of Jesus in a more readable manner. (Collections of wisdom sayings are widely attested in Jewish and Christian literature; see in the Nag Hammadi library alone *The Sentences of Sextus* and *The Teachings of Silvanus*.) The "dialogues" with Jesus remained popular for centuries in some Christian Gnostic circles, but the narrative Gospels outshone both sayings collections and dialogues by incorporating both those forms into compelling dramas.

Words attributed to Jesus in *Savior* and *James* often are typical of the early tradition. The idea of "seek and find" is a response of Jesus in *Savior*: "And [let] him who [. . .] seek and find and [rejoice]." Not only that, the saying represents in *Savior* an organizing theme for the questioning by the three disciples—Judas, Matthew, and Mary. They have sought, found, and marveled, but their ruling and resting will come in the future.

In *James*, the Lord sometimes speaks in a manner similar to the Jesus in the synoptic Gospels—"the kingdom of heaven is like an ear of grain . . .," "the Word is like a grain of wheat when someone had sown it . . ." and "let not the Kingdom of Heaven wither, for it is like a palm shoot . . ." In separate studies, Ron Cameron and Charles Hedrick have proposed that some of these sayings may have derived from the early Jesus tradition.

Both Nag Hammadi texts refer to sayings of Jesus by phrases or "names." In *Savior* 53, Mary refers to three sayings: "the wickedness of each day," "the laborer is worthy of his food," and "the disciple resembles his teacher." Parallels to each one can be found in Matthew (6:34b; 10:10b; and 10:25), but Luke also has two of them. Matthew and Luke (thus Q) and 1 Timothy 5:18b all say "the laborer deserves his wages." The early (turn of the first century) Christian document *Didache* (13:1–2) comes closest to *Savior* when it says the prophet or teacher "is worthy, like the workman, of his food."

In *James*, the resurrected and glorified Lord asks James and Peter why they compelled him to extend his earthly appearances another eighteen days "for the sake of the parables."* Jesus tells James and Peter: "It was enough for some ⟨to listen⟩ to the teaching and understand 'The Shepherds' and 'The Seed' and 'The Building' and 'The Lamps of the Virgins' and 'The Wage of the Workmen' and 'The Didrachmae' and 'The Woman.' " It is uncertain here which parables the author has in mind in each case, except perhaps Matthew 25:1–12 for "The Lamps of the Virgins" and Luke 15:8–10 for "The Didrachmae," which is usually called "the lost coin" parable today.

Not only are the two dialogues rooted in Jesus sayings prevalent in the first century, but they appear to have been written without knowledge of the New Testament Gospels. Pagels and Koester wrote in their 1988 introduction to the *Dialogue of the Savior* that the text has sayings with parallels in the Gospels of Matthew, Luke, and John, and particularly in *The Gospel of Thomas*. "However, a literary dependence upon any of these writings seems unlikely," they write. The dialogues are similar to those in the Gospel of John but "less advanced and theologically less complex than the Johannine parallels," leading Pagels and Koester to suggest that the basic source incorporated into *Savior* was written before the end of the first century.

The Apocryphon of James likewise is comparable to the Gospel of John in its use of sayings and discourses, wrote Cameron in *The Other Gospels* (1982) and in *Sayings Traditions in the Apocryphon*

---

*There is conjecture that "days" should have read "months." The introduction to *James* speaks of Jesus continuing his resurrection appearances for 550 days since he rose from the dead. That contrasts to the 40 days post-resurrection period in the New Testament's Acts but approximates the time claimed by the apocryphal *Ascension of Isaiah*.

of James (1984). He calls it an early Christian writing based on an independent sayings collection contemporary with other such Jesus sayings collections. The introduction depicts the disciples remembering what Jesus had taught them and writing it into books—a literary motif characteristic of the first half of the second century, according to Cameron.

Both texts had final authors who preferred the title "Savior" over "the Lord," the appellation apparently found in their basic sources. In *Savior*, "Savior" is used only at the beginning and very end of the text and at a seam connecting the author's composition with one of his five sources. The dialogue source still accounts for 65 percent of the text, according to Pagels and Koester.

In *James*, Jesus is called "Savior" frequently in the introductory section ("the Lord" and "Jesus" once each) and one time near the very end. Noting that similar pattern in *Savior*, Cameron says the dialogues and discourses of "the Lord" in three-fourths of *James* constitute the original part. The editor, Cameron says, prefaced the work with an introduction that made it appear as if it were a "letter" from James. The "letter" answered a request for "a secret book which was revealed to me and Peter" (as opposed to the rest of the disciples). At least the last two sentences of *James* appear to have also been added by the editor, but Cameron did not attempt to separate out secondary material at the text's conclusion.

Cameron disagrees with the earlier thesis of Pheme Perkins that *The Apocryphon of James* was written sometime after 200 C.E. Perkins argues that far from being a non-Gnostic book as many have thought, *James* is instead "a sustained and vigorous attack on orthodox attempts to eradicate Gnosticism." She contends, in *The Gnostic Dialogue* and in articles, that James often depends on or reacts to the Gospel of John and that it shows a knowledge of Irenaeus's anti-Gnostic writings.

A late date is also preferred by Francis E. Williams, who translated and introduced the text for *The Nag Hammadi Library in English*. He allows for the possibility of its composition before 150 C.E., but also claims to detect a "large amount of typically Gnostic terminology." Williams states flatly, "It is clear that the persons for whom this tractate was written made a distinction between themselves and the larger Christian church." Yet he concedes that questions about the document's literary history deserve further investigation.

If that is so, it's because so many features of *The Apocryphon of James* reflect first-century perspectives. Affinities exist in the names of central figures, the language of salvation, the treatment of faith, and the presentation of a mystical experience.

—The names of central figures: "The Lord" is generally acknowledged to be one of the oldest titles for the risen Jesus. He is never called Christ here—or in *The Dialogue of the Savior, The Gospel of Thomas*, or Q. By contrast, it is rare to find the name Christ missing from a later Christian Gnostic writing that focuses on Jesus.

Also, James, the head of the Jerusalem church, is given no laudatory title, not even the popular "James the Just." Even the New Testament's Letter of James opens by calling him "a servant of God and of the Lord." The second-century James literature— whether orthodox or Gnostic Christian—tends to praise James to the skies. The introduction and closing sentences of *The Apocryphon of James* give James a preferred status, to be sure. At the end, James sends the envious disciples on assignments elsewhere as he departs for Jerusalem. But the text's central dialogue treats James and Peter as approximate equals in receiving the teachings of the risen Lord. If Mark and the other Gospels are correct, James, the brother of Jesus, was not a follower of Jesus in his lifetime and not a witness to his resurrection and thereby would seem unlikely to merit special teachings. Yet James's central role in *The Apocryphon of James* is consistent with the early tradition known to Paul. One of the oldest Christian creeds says that Jesus was buried, was raised on the third day, and he appeared to Cephas (Peter), then to the Twelve, then simultaneously to five hundred brethren, then to James, then to all the apostles (1 Cor. 15:3–7). At another point, Paul says somewhat sarcastically, that Peter, James, and John are the "pillars of the church" (1 Gal. 2:9).

—The language of salvation: Paul expresses mock wonderment at those in the Corinthian church who apparently favored a wisdom-oriented salvation. "Already you are filled! Already you have become rich! Without us you have become king! And would that you did reign, so that we might share the rule with you!" (1 Cor. 4:8) In *James,* Jesus is presented as saying that no one enters the kingdom of heaven at his bidding, but only if they have been "filled." The exhortations to James and Peter do not state with what one is to be filled, but it is clear that salvation is at stake. Jesus also makes reference to the disciples being healed so they might "reign." But Jesus says it is not easy. "Verily I say unto you, it is easier for a pure one to fall into defilement and for a man of light to fall into darkness, than for you to reign or not to reign." *James* does not use the term "rich" although the text refers to the outsiders who will not receive "the Father's inheritance." The term "rich" is prominent elsewhere in wisdom literature, the genre that informs both *James* and *Thomas.* Jesus says in *Thomas* 81, "Let him who has grown rich be king, and let him who possesses power renounce it." The wise man is both "rich" and reigning as a "king."

—Faith: Jesus says in *James,* right after sayings in which he describes himself as the elusive figure of Wisdom:

Blessed will they be who have known me; woe to those who have heard and have not believed! Blessed will they be who have not seen [yet have believed]!

The last of these blessings appears in the Gospel of John, which immortalized the expression "doubting Thomas." The Gospel depicts Thomas as skeptical about the other disciples' claims that Jesus had risen from the dead. Jesus challenges Thomas to place his fingers on his wounds, whereupon Thomas exclaims, "My Lord and my God!" Despite that exalted statement of belief, Jesus says to Thomas (John 20:29): "Have you believed because you have seen me? Blessed are those who have not seen and yet believe."

The story is normally recounted in church as if it were an actual, remembered event. But most critical scholars treat it as a story composed for theological reasons. At any rate, Koester claims, "The secondary usage of the saying in John's Gospel is obvious, whereas *The Apocryphon of James* has preserved the saying in its more original setting of a sayings collection which was expanded into a discourse of Jesus."

—Mystical experience: *James* describes an "ascent" into three heavens by James and Peter that is compatible with the supernatural world of Paul and the practices of the earliest Christians. After Jesus departed from them, Peter and James bent their knees in prayer.

I and Peter . . . gave thanks and sent our heart(s) upwards to heaven. We heard with our ears, and saw with our eyes, the noise of wars and a trumpet blare and a great turmoil. And when we had passed beyond that place, we sent our mind(s) farther upwards and saw with our eyes and heard with our ears hymns and angelic benedictions and angelic rejoicing. And heavenly majesties were singing praises, and we too rejoiced. After this again, we wished to send our spirit upward to the Majesty, and after ascending we were not permitted to see or hear anything . . .

James and Peter were denied the sights and sounds of the third and highest heaven, *James* says, because the other disciples broke their concentration with questions about what Jesus had said to them and where he went.

The ascent described in *The Apocryphon of James* may represent a spiritual exercise attempted by early Jesus believers. Paul, indicating to the Corinthians that he too has had ecstatic spiritual experiences, says that fourteen years earlier (perhaps only a dozen years after Jesus' crucifixion) he was "caught up" into the third heaven—whether in the body or out of body, he couldn't say (2 Cor. 12). Both *James* and Paul avoid describing what was visible in the highest heaven. It should be noted that many apocalyptic writings (Jewish, Gnostic, and Christian) speak of seven heavens, not three.

Thomas 11a also seems to suggest that the third heaven is the ultimate goal: "This heaven will pass away and the one above it will pass away." This may be simply a variant on a saying attributed to Jesus that "heaven and earth will pass away, but my words will not pass away" (Mark 13:30–31; Matt. 24:34–35). But some other *Thomas* sayings hint at a promised heavenly vision, especially saying 15: "When you see one who was not born of woman, prostrate yourselves on your faces and worship him. That one is your father."

Both Paul and *Thomas* use a saying about what the eye will see and the ear will hear, an expression widespread in antiquity apparently referring to heavenly secrets, if not visions. Paul quotes an unknown source: "What no eye has seen, nor ear heard, nor the heart of man conceived, what God has prepared for those who love him" (1 Cor. 2:9). Jesus, speaking with the voice of Wisdom, promises in *Thomas* 17: "I shall give you what no eye has seen and what no ear has heard and what no hand has touched and what has never occurred to the human mind" (see Isa. 64:4 and Luke 10:23–24/Matt. 13:16–17.)

Studies of *The Dialogue of the Savior*, *The Apocryphon of James*, and *The Gospel of Thomas* have increasingly shown that they contain striking similarities. And, most important for dating purposes, they share sayings, terminology, and ideas found in other likely first-century writings. A reference book invaluable for comparing these parallels was published in 1985—*New Gospel Parallels*, Volume 2, *John and the Other Gospels*, designed and edited by Robert W. Funk.

Koester, editor of *Harvard Theological Review*, wrote in an article for that journal in 1980 that *Thomas*, *The Dialogue of the Savior*, and *The Apocryphon of James* "are doubtlessly early Christian gospels" in the broad sense of the word. Together with fragments of two other narrative gospels—*The Gospel of Peter*, discovered in 1866, and an "unknown gospel" called *Papyrus Egerton 2*, discovered in 1935—Koester said "they are at least as old and as valuable as the canonical gospels as sources for the earliest developments of the traditions about Jesus. . . . The term apocryphal with all its negative connotations should not prejudice us any longer."

Whether *Thomas*, *James*, and *Savior* can be called "Gnostic" in their orientation has been a matter of debate. All three texts speak of potential believers needing to return to their heavenly "place." The "place of life" is sought in *Savior* and *Thomas*. The idea of spiritual roots to which one must return was present in Sethian and Valentinian Gnostic writings. But the evil archon, the lower God of Gnostic myth, does not appear in these three works. In *James*, for instance, a rather traditional Christian reference is made to the evil one, who is also called Satan and the devil.

The *Thomas* literature, starting with *The Gospel of Thomas*, does not fit into the usual definitions of Gnosticism, writes Layton in *The Gnostic Scriptures*. "Instead, it presupposes only an uncomplicated Hellenistic myth of the divine origins of the self; conceives of god as unitary; does not discuss the error of wisdom; puts no stress on revisionistic retelling of the myth of Genesis; and does not teach about an ignorant maker of the world," Layton says.

The lack of Gnostic flags in *Thomas* did not deter Robert M. Wilson to label it Gnostic—despite the fact that "much of the book indeed could be read by any orthodox Christian without suspicion." Wilson said the purpose may have been Gnostic propaganda "designed to lure the unsuspecting away from orthodoxy into the ranks of heresy." The first few commentaries on *Thomas* presumed that a Gnostic wrote it. Previously unknown sayings of Jesus or variations on a familiar saying were usually interpreted then as carrying an esoteric Gnostic meaning.

A full-fledged rebuttal of that view was published in 1983 by Stevan L. Davies in *The Gospel of Thomas and Christian Wisdom*. Davies maintains that *Thomas* was not Gnostic in any meaningful sense. Rather, he says, its concepts and terms could be explained as deriving from the Jewish and Christian wisdom traditions. Davies, who dated the composition between 50 and 70 C.E., says *Thomas* stands at the beginning of Christian theological speculation and therefore is naive and unsystematic. Few Nag Hammadi specialists, however, have ruled out some Gnostic or proto-Gnostic additions to the text.

By the mid-1980s, *The Gospel of Thomas* had continued to fascinate a growing number of scholars and earn respect from most of them. In surveying the state of New Testament studies in a February 27, 1985, lecture at Princeton Theological Seminary, James H. Charlesworth, a scholar not directly involved in Nag Hammadi studies, said there was "phenomenal" interest in *Thomas*. "I have counted 397 publications on it alone," said Charlesworth, editor of the two-volume *Pseudepigrapha of the Old Testament*, the Jewish sacred literature written in the period between the Old and New Testaments. He said he considered the New Testament scholar's central task to "seek what can be known about the life and teachings of Jesus of Nazareth."

The Gospel of Thomas is significant in the search for the historical Jesus for three reasons, Charlesworth said. Not only is it a text reminiscent of the lost source (Q) used independently by

Luke and Matthew and containing at least some sayings independent of the canonical Gospels, but also "it is now becoming well recognized that it is improper to discard *The Gospel of Thomas* as late, derivative, and gnostic," he said.

17. The Gospel of Thomas

It is surely ironical that a gospel credited to Thomas has turned doubters into believers. Skepticism normally serves historical-critical scholarship well, but it proved misplaced when many first scoffed at the historical value of *The Gospel of Thomas*.

By 1976 French scholar Jacques E. Menard could write in the *Interpreter's Dictionary of the Bible, Supplementary Volume*, that "about half" of the *Thomas* sayings were not rewritten versions of those in Mark, Matthew, and Luke and had a claim to authenticity. Harold W. Attridge of Notre Dame, writing in the 1985 *Harper's Bible Dictionary*, concurred on the independent sources of *Thomas*. Regarding the previously unknown sayings of Jesus, Attridge said some were probably composed by believers drawing on "the traditions of Israel's wisdom literature." But some of the new sayings "are as likely to be authentic sayings of Jesus as those in many canonical texts," Attridge wrote.

Menard did not challenge an oft-presumed composition date for *Thomas* of 140 C.E., but Attridge said a first-century date "cannot be excluded." No scholar, however, has gone so far as to propose that the disciple Thomas was the actual author. In fact—irony of ironies—there are grounds for doubting that the name Thomas was originally a part of this sayings collection.

By examining "who's who" in *The Gospel of Thomas*, some scholars see revealing signs of when the text took its final form and why. A pair of sayings praise James the Just (more accurately, "the righteous") and the disciple Thomas above all the other followers of Jesus:

(12) The disciples said to Jesus, "We know that you will depart from us. Who is to be our leader?"

Jesus said to them, "Wherever you are, you are to go to James the righteous, for whose sake heaven and earth came into being."

(13) Jesus said to his disciples, "Compare me to someone and tell me whom I am like."

Simon Peter said to him, "You are like a righteous angel."

Matthew said to him, "You are like a wise philosopher."

Thomas said to him, "Master, my mouth is wholly incapable of saying whom you are like."

Jesus said, "I am not your master. Because you have drunk, you have become intoxicated from the bubbling spring which I have measured out."

And he took him and withdrew and told him three things. When Thomas returned to his companions, they asked him, "What did Jesus say to you?"

Thomas said to them, "If I tell you one of the things which he told me, you will pick up stones and throw them at me; a fire will come out of the stones and burn you up."

James, the brother of Jesus and head of the Jerusalem church, is acknowledged as the ecclesiastical leader in *Thomas* 12. The "description of James as one 'for whose sake heaven and earth came into being' is a Jewish expression used to praise holy people," observes Marvin W. Meyer. Because the question and answer seem so purposefully designed to signify James's leadership, few, if any, scholars would suggest that this was a remembered exchange with Jesus, even if it is conceivable that Jesus had left such instructions.

In saying 13, Thomas is presented as the disciple with the highest awe of Jesus and the one favored as the repository for secret knowledge. The combination of sayings 12 and 13 suggests to Helmut Koester "a politico-ecclesiastical situation in Palestine" in the first century rather than a controversy in a later period.

"Appeals to particular apostolic authorities are well known in the second and third generations of Christianity," says Koester. Some New Testament texts written in the last third of the first century bear the names of authorities who have already passed from the scene. Koester cites 2 Thessalonians as a Letter "closely imitating the first letter of Paul to his congregation" but trying to settle an argument in which Paul's authority was being quoted by both sides in a dispute. In the same way, the Letters of John were written to affirm and interpret the authority of John transmitted in the Gospel under his name, Koester says.

But "a most direct parallel" to the juxtaposition of *Thomas* 12 and 13, Koester says, occurs in the last chapter of John. John 21, widely considered an addition to the original gospel, establishes in effect Peter as the leader of the church through Jesus' command to him, "Tend my sheep!" (John 21:15–17). "The Johannine churches thus recognize the ecclesiastical authority of Peter, just as the Thomas community acknowledges the authority of James," Koester writes.

Comparable to the favor enjoyed by Thomas in *Thomas* 13 is the position John 21 accorded to the unnamed "disciple whom Jesus loved" (21:7). The beloved disciple's status is mysteriously expressed (21:21–23) and he is credited as the author of the whole Gospel (21:24).

Peter is the foremost figure in most of the New Testament. In Mark he gives the right answer to Jesus' question of "Who do men say that I am?"—"You are the Christ"—although Jesus quickly rebukes Peter as "Satan" for objecting to Jesus' prophecy of his fate (Mark 8:27–33). The Gospel of Matthew softens Mark's rebuke of Peter by having Jesus bestow enormous authority on Peter: "On this rock I will build my church . . . I will give you the keys to the kingdom . . . " (Matt. 16:18–19).

Peter fares poorly in *Thomas*. In addition to inadequately comparing Jesus to "a righteous angel" in 12, "Simon Peter" is countermanded by Jesus in 114 when he urges that Mary leave them. Note that it is simply "Thomas" in 12 and in the title, *Gospel According to Thomas*, which immediately follows 114.

The name Thomas also occurs at the beginning of the text, but here it is a combined name. He is called "Didymos Judas Thomas" in the prologue to the Coptic text found near Nag Hammadi. He is identified as "[Judas, who is] also Thomas" in the prologue of the Greek fragment found at Oxyrhynchus, Egypt. Otherwise, the prologue's wording is the same— "these are the secret sayings of the living Jesus which . . . wrote down."

The combination of "Judas Thomas" is found nowhere in the New Testament; the names appear only separately. A disciple called Thomas appears in the lists of twelve disciples in the synoptic Gospels. Thomas is the hellenized spelling of the Aramaic "Toma," which means "twin." The Greek word for "twin," didymos, is added redundantly as a nickname for Thomas on three occasions in the Gospel of John (11:16; 14:5; and 21:2). Only in the Syriac version of the Gospel of John, at 14:22, does the name Judas Thomas appear. In Greek manuscripts containing John 14:22, and thus in standard English translations, that person is called "Judas (not the Iscariot)." Aside from this Judas and the Judas called the betrayer of Jesus in the four Gospels, there are two other Judases in the tradition. One is "Judas the son of James," whom Luke (6:16; Acts 1:13) counts as one of the twelve disciples. The other is Judas, the brother of Jesus (Mark 6:3; Matt. 13:55; Jude 1:1).

Judas the brother must be the one in mind in John 14:22, if the antagonistic question posed is any guide. "Judas (not the Iscariot)" asks why Jesus doesn't reveal his divine nature to the world. The same objection was voiced by Jesus' "brothers" (unnamed), who urged Jesus to go to Judea to show off his works to his disciples. "For no man works in secret if he seeks to be known openly," the brothers told Jesus. "If you do these things, show yourself to the world." The Gospel then adds pointedly: "For even his brothers did not believe in him" (John 7:3–5). Jesus, dying on the cross, even declares that the beloved disciple is now the son of his mother, and the Gospel says the disciple took her into his home (John 19:26–27)—surely one last slap at Jesus' natural brothers. And the disciple Thomas, even before his doubting encounter with the risen Jesus in John 20, utters a dumb statement at 11:16 and asks a dim-witted question at 14:5.

The Gospel of John certainly discredits "the brothers" of Jesus as nonbelievers. But, as shown above, two other followers of Jesus portrayed as skeptics are "Judas (not the Iscariot)" and the disciple Thomas. Was the author of John covering all the bases, so to speak, by casting aspersions on "the brothers" and on two possible names for the brother with the reputed secret understanding? This suggests the possibility that the names Judas and Thomas came together before the time the Gospel of John reached its final stage.

Remarkably, the Gospel of John's statement that the brothers did not believe in Jesus usually goes unchallenged by modern scholars. However, it may be that they simply believed less about Jesus than later churches and Gospel authors did. The brothers of Jesus clearly enjoyed great privileges in the 50s, according to Paul. Paul complained to the Corinth church that the other apostles and "the brothers of the Lord and Cephas [Peter]" were accompanied in their travels by wives. Paul and his co-workers Barnabas, he added, had to work in order to pay their way (1 Cor. 9:5–6).

The Syrian church in Edessa regarded "Judas Thomas" as its founding apostle. In the long and legendary *Acts of Thomas*, which tells of the apostle's missionary travels to India, he is specifically called the twin brother of Jesus.

He is also mentioned in the so-called Abgar legend of the Edessan church. Correspondence was supposedly exchanged between Jesus and King Abgar V of Edessa (9–46 C.E.), in which the latter appealed to Jesus to heal him. Jesus said he would send one of his disciples after he had completed his mission. Appended to the letters was a note saying that "Judas who was called Thomas" sent the apostle Thaddeus, one of the seventy, to heal the king.

In the previously unknown *Book of Thomas*, found in the Nag Hammadi cache, the disciple is referred to frequently as "Thomas" (and "Brother Thomas" and "my brother Thomas" by the Savior), but also as "Judas Thomas" and once as "Judas— the one called Thomas."

Koester suggests that Judas was the original name of Thomas. "The identity of Judas, the brother of the Lord, with Thomas is more likely a primitive tradition than a later confusion," Koester writes. The Harvard professor says it is possible that memory of that name derives from the actual, historical activity of the apostle in Edessa or his activity in another area of Palestine-Syria from which the church in Edessa owed its beginnings. Koester doubts what seems to him the only alternate explanation—that Thomas was the original name and someone "appropriated the name of one of the brothers of Jesus," adding Judas to Thomas.

A variation on Koester's first explanation should be considered: that Judas was indeed the original name but that Judas was *never* known additionally as Thomas until this sayings collection underwent editing. This accounts for the consistent identification of Judas in *The Dialogue of the Savior* simply as Judas. *The Dialogue of the Savior* and *Thomas* are very much alike in their Gnostic-like jargon and theology, such as referring to believers as "the solitaries" and to the heavenly "places" where they should return.* Yet *The Dialogue of the Savior* refers to Judas sixteen times without ever attaching another name. Nor does the biblical Letter of Jude attach the name Thomas.

Here is how the names Judas and Thomas might have merged:

1. The secret sayings of Jesus in this collection were attributed originally to "Judas," and may have been set down about the same time as the Q collection—the middle of the first century. The introduction appeared to be the only identification for the writing at one time. James Robinson notes approvingly that Martin Krause's early analysis suggests that "the introduction to *The Gospel of Thomas,* defining the work as a collection of sayings, is more primitive than the subscription, which designates it as a gospel."

2. But the users of this sayings collection encounter trouble when the Gospel of Mark becomes widely known and used, for the story says that Judas and other brothers did not believe Jesus was so wonderful (Mark 6:4). Indeed, Jesus' family was embarrassed by its reputedly demon-possessed member (3:21–22). Not only that, the only Judas among the disciples is identified as the betrayer of Jesus.

(The modern reader may protest, "Well, everybody knew then there were at least two Judases—the infamous one and the brother of Jesus, who never became a disciple!" But *The Dialogue of the Savior* acts as if Judas was a disciple and Jude is remembered well in early tradition, as was his brother James. Mark apparently influenced the other three New Testament Gospel writers to follow suit in implying that the brothers rejected Jesus when he was alive. This did force the church, however, to say that somehow all was forgiven very quickly—to the point of giving them prominent places in the early church!)

3. The community that used the Judas sayings collections was perhaps being misunderstood as devotees of Judas Iscariot. They

---

*Two other disciples who figure in *Thomas* 13 and 114 are Matthew and Mary—and they are the other two disciples named with Judas in *The Dialogue of the Savior.* Matthew and Mary come out better than Peter in *Thomas.* Matthew's characterization of Jesus as a wise philosopher in *Thomas* 13 is at least close to the presentation of Jesus in sayings collections and Mary is defended in *Thomas* 114 as worthy of salvation although she is not inherently the equal of males.

The Gospel of Thomas, whose title can be seen centered on the right hand page, was a part of Codex II, held open by Marianne Doresse. Later the papyrus sheets were cut down the middle to place each page between sheets of plexiglass for preservation. Photo courtesy of The Institute for Antiquity and Christianity.

would have to explain constantly not only that this was Judas *the brother* but also that their understanding (in spite of the synoptic Gospels) was that both brothers were followers of Jesus during his lifetime.

4. Looking at Mark's (or Luke's, or Matthew's) list of the twelve disciples, our possibly beleaguered community could see that one of the names, Thomas, is virtually a nickname, "twin." The community loyal to the sayings authority of Judas, positive that Judas was a disciple, may have reasoned that he went under this nickname—perhaps because he reputedly looked enough like Jesus to be his twin. (It is only much later in the Syrian church that Judas is flatly called the "twin" of Jesus.)

5. The introduction, or prologue, of the text is changed to identify the source as "Judas, who is also Thomas." The Coptic

copy of *Thomas* pushes Judas and Thomas together and adds "Didymos" for good measure.

6. The powerful impact of Mark's "Gospel," and maybe of other narrative Gospels as well, prompts the editor to call the sayings collection "The Gospel of Thomas" despite the different format. But in adding the title and saying 13, the editor takes no further chances that people would misidentify the authority figure. He omits the name Judas and uses just "Thomas."

Obviously, if that editing scenario is correct, it means that those who used *The Dialogue of the Savior* felt no similar compulsion to change that text. But the above solution was ingenious, if true, and it cannot be assumed the same idea would occur to other communities or be seen as necessary.

Another question: if Judas was the only name on the original version of *Thomas*, could it have actually been written down by him? His brother James met a martyr's death about 62 C.E., but it is unknown how long Judas lived. Paul indicates that brothers of Jesus were living in the 50s, but he does not identify them (1 Cor. 9:5). Little tradition has survived for the activity of any brothers other than Judas and James. Scholars remain agnostic on the actual compiler of the sayings for lack of evidence.

Rather than the *authority* credited for transmission of the sayings, the *content* of *The Gospel of Thomas* (a title that will stick) was what attracted the interest of most New Testament scholars. One is the late Norman Perrin of the University of Chicago Divinity School. Without immersing himself in Gnostic studies, Perrin was still able to make frequent use of *Thomas* in his 1967 book *Rediscovering the Teaching of Jesus*. "Much of the material in [*Thomas*] has clearly been either modified or created to serve a gnostic Christian purpose," Perrin writes. But by the same token the canonical Gospels also were "either modified or created to serve orthodox Christian purposes," he says.

As a working hypothesis in his search for authentic sayings of Jesus, Perrin assumes, like Koester, that the *Thomas* sayings were from a source independent of Q or Mark, Matthew, and Luke. The hypothesis seemed to work. For one thing, he says, the order of sayings in *Thomas* does not follow any sequence found in the New Testament Gospels.

A more telling indication, however, "is the fact that over and over again the text of a parable in *Thomas* will be different" from its counterpart in the New Testament, he says. And the *Thomas* rendition appears to be the more basic, less elaborated variety, he adds. Because of that, Perrin suggests that the Nag Hammadi text contains examples of Jesus' sayings that are closer to the likely authentic teaching than the synoptic equivalents.

As an illustration, Perrin cites no. 64, the longest "saying" in *Thomas*:

(64) Jesus said, "A man had received visitors. And when he had pre-pared the dinner, he sent his servant to invite the guests. He went to the first one and said to him, 'My master invites you.' He said, 'I have claims against some merchants. They are coming to me this evening. I must go and give them my orders. I ask to be excused from the dinner.' He went to another and said to him, 'My master has invited you.' He said to him, 'I have just bought a house and am required for the day. I shall not have any spare time.' He went to another and said to him, 'My master invites you.' He said to him 'My friend is going to get mar-ried, and I am prepared the banquet. I shall not be able to come. I ask to be excused from the dinner.' He went to another and said to him, 'My master invites you.' He said to him, 'I have just bought a farm, and I am on my way to collect the rent. I shall not be able to come. I ask to be excused.' The servant returned and said to his master, 'Those whom you invited to the dinner have asked to be excused.' The master said to his servant, 'Go outside to the streets and bring back those whom you happen to meet, so that they may dine.' Businessmen and mer-chants [will] not enter the places of my father."

The same parable is told differently by Matthew (22:1–14) and Luke (14:16–24), and they differ between themselves. Matthew's feast giver is a king, and the dinner is a marriage feast, sym-bolizing God and the age to come in Jewish imagery of the time, according to Perrin. Matthew's servants are the Christian "ser-vants of God," but they are rejected, then killed, representing the treatment they received from Jews. The king, angry at this, sends his troops to destroy the city—"certainly a reference to the destruction of Jerusalem by the Romans interpreted as the judg-ment of God upon the Jews, all in accordance with early Chris-tian apologetic," Perrin says. Finally, Matthew adds an epilogue about a guest who came without a wedding garment, that is, he was unprepared for the coming age.

Luke's version is about "a man" who gave a banquet. It tends to shape the story along the themes of his Gospel and the book of Acts, which he also wrote. The servant is sent out three times—to the original guests (Jews), to the poor and handicapped in the city (Jewish outcasts), and to the persons on the highway outside the city (Gentiles). "Matthew and Luke have both understood the story as having reference to the missionary situation of the church, and in particular to the situation created by the success of the Gentile mission," Perrin writes.

It is hard to resist the conclusion, suggests Perrin, that the story of the dinner guests in *Thomas* is nearer to the teaching of Jesus than Matthew or Luke. "It does not reflect the situation of the church, nor, except for the generalizing conclusion, is it at all concerned with anything specifically Gnostic." The conclusion in *Thomas*—"Businessmen and merchants [will] not enter the places of my father"—is taken by Perrin to be a Gnostic rejection of the material world. Noting that stories grow and develop in the telling and retelling, Perrin says the parable in *Thomas*, except for the excuses and the last sentence, "is in all respects the simplest and least developed version."

Many of Jesus' parables, both in the New Testament Gospels and in *Thomas*, strive to make the point that the kingdom of God is such a surprise and a joy to those who discover it that they abandon less important things and concentrate on the newfound treasure. The parables about "the treasure in the field" and "the pearl" are just such examples. Matthew placed the two together (13:44–46). *Thomas* has versions of both, but they are widely separated.

Perrin says the same point is made by *Thomas* 8, which he regards as a "new," previously unknown parable:

And he said, "The man is like a wise fisherman who cast his net into the sea and drew it up from the sea full of small fish. Among them the wise fisherman found a fine large fish. He threw all the small fish back into the sea and chose the large fish without difficulty. Whoever has ears to hear, let him hear."

Opinion is divided on the "newness" of the parable. Some believe it is not distinctive, merely the *Thomas* version of the fisherman's dragnet parable in Matthew 13:47.

Thomas 8 also includes a widely used saying in the Jesus tradition, "Whoever has ears to hear, let him hear." In one wording or another, the line occurs six times in *Thomas*, three in Matthew, twice each in Mark and Luke, and many times in the New Testament book of Revelation.

Perrin, in some cases, accepts the judgment of early commentators on *The Gospel of Thomas* who tended to read some familiar Jesus parables through Gnostic lenses. Thus, Perrin accepts Bertil Gartner's interpretation of *Thomas* 96 as a saying transformed to serve Gnostic aims. No. 96 reads, "The kingdom of the father is like [a certain] woman. She took a little leaven, [concealed] it in some dough, and made it into large loaves. Let him who has ears hear." The Q version of the saying (Matt. 13:33; Luke 13:20–21) says a woman took and hid the leaven "in three measures of flour, till it was all leavened." Citing Gartner's *The Theology of the Gospel According to Thomas*, Perrin says the *Thomas* version produces large loaves "and the leaven now equals the heavenly particle of light, the spiritual element within man which makes salvation possible." It could also be argued, however, that *Thomas* 96 is simply another "growth" parable such as the widely used "mustard seed" parable (*Thomas* 20; Mark 4:30–32; Matt. 13:31–32; and Luke 13:18–19).

The following two parables in *Thomas*, 97 and 98, are clearly new discoveries in the Jesus tradition. They are found nowhere else in either the New Testament or other Christian literature.

(97) Jesus said, "The kingdom of the [father] is like a certain woman who was carrying a [jar] full of meal. While she was walking [on the] road, still some distance from home, the handle of the jar broke and the meal emptied out behind her [on] the road. She did not realize it; she had noticed no accident. When she reached her house, she set the jar down and found it empty."

(98) Jesus said, "The kingdom of the father is like a certain man who wanted to kill a powerful man. In his house he drew his sword and stuck it into the wall in order to find out whether his hand could carry through. Then he slew the powerful man."

Neither parable is a likely candidate today for fresh sermon material, even if a pastor could surmount the hurdle of introducing parables from an apocryphal, noncanonical source.

Thomas 97 seems innocuous, though it must be realized that

Jesus' comparisons to the "kingdom" are not all easily explained. In this case, the point may be that the kingdom can slip away unnoticed.

Thomas 98, speaking to the wisdom of preparation, is chilling in its detached description of an assassin. Yet the Jesus sayings tradition does contain stories of violence or suggestions of violence, such as the parable of the evil tenant farmers (*Thomas* 65; Mark 12:1–12, Matt. 21:33–46; and Luke 20:9–19). Perrin considers "the assassin" an authentic parable, comparing its emphasis on preparation to Luke 14:28–32. He also declares "the extreme unlikelihood of anyone but Jesus using a Zealot assassin as an example."

Well before the Nag Hammadi find, historical-critical New Testament studies assumed that many sayings of Jesus often took unintended meanings because they were used to serve a Gospel's story line. *Thomas* sayings frequently reinforce that perception. One example is *Thomas* 78, which starts with the question, "Why have you come out into the desert?" The word "desert" could be translated "wilderness." In Q's version of this saying (Matt. 11:7; Luke 7:24), the context is Jesus is referring to John the Baptist, a man associated with the wilderness. There is no such reference to the Baptist in *Thomas*.

Another example is *Thomas* 79, which seems natural as one unit, instead of two as in Luke:

(79) A woman from the crowd said to him, "Blessed are the womb which bore you and the breasts which nourished you."
He said to [her], "Blessed are those who have heard the word of the father and have truly kept it.
"For there will be days when you will say, 'Blessed are the womb which has not conceived and the breasts which have not given milk.' "

Luke 11:27–28 contains essentially the first two parts. The prophetic third line is found in Luke 23:29 as part of the precrucifixion scene. Taken together, as it reads in *Thomas*, the pronouncement is not only a plea to focus on the message and not the man. It also reflects an idea contained elsewhere in *Thomas* and the Synoptics—that the natural family is inferior to the new spiritual family of the kingdom (*Thomas* 16, 55, 99, 101, 105). *Thomas* 105 radically states the case: "He who knows the father and the mother will be called the son of a harlot." Yet 55 and 101, similar sayings, say that no one may be a disciple to Jesus unless they "hate" mother and father—the same verb used in the saying in Luke (14:26). Perrin, who does not comment on the *Thomas* versions, says Luke 14:26 "may be regarded as authentic. . . . It vividly illustrates the obedience required" to Jesus' challenge.

One noticeable difference between *Thomas* and the synoptic Gospels is that whoever compiled the sayings in *Thomas* had no apocalyptic expectations and eschewed the title "Son of man." There are nearly seventy-five references to the Son of man in Mark, Matthew, and Luke—most of them bearing apocalyptic connotations. When duplication is allowed for, there are thirty-seven distinct sayings about the Son of man, according to one count.

Thomas uses the expression once, but it is in the common, roundabout Jewish manner of saying "man." *Thomas* 86 reads: "[The foxes have their holes] and the birds have their nests, but the son of man has no place to lay his head and rest." That saying also appeared in Q—see Matthew 8:20 and Luke 9:58. It may refer in Q to the insecurities of an itinerant ministry, a strong theme in that work as generally reconstructed. But standing alone, the saying has the cast of a proverbial reflection on human experience.

The Jesus of *The Gospel of Thomas* admonishes his disciples not to expect the kingdom to come in the clouds or in the distant future. *Thomas* 3 and 113 present Jesus saying that the kingdom is present in the world, both in and around the hearers. Before the discovery of *Thomas*, this teaching was preserved only in Luke 17:20—"Behold, the kingdom of God is in the midst of you."*

By contrast, in the New Testament, the basic thrust of the Pauline and Gospel writings is to look ahead apocalyptically to the coming kingdom, sometimes conceived as Jesus returning as

---

*Thomas 51 and 91 have Jesus saying words that resemble the admonition of Lady Wisdom in Jewish literature that she is present in the world yet humans fail to recognize that, but the motif is pronounced in such sayings as *Thomas* 28 and 38 where Jesus speaks either with the voice of Wisdom or as the embodiment of Wisdom. The compiler of the sayings in *Thomas* probably went beyond authentic Jesus sources to create these four sayings of a wisdom nature.

the glorified Son of man. The synoptics also contain Jesus sayings that emphasize the present. But a number of American scholars are convinced that this mixture came from the grafting of apocalyptic-style beliefs onto an earlier wisdom stratum of sayings attributed to Jesus. The tendency now is to see Q as a collection that had an initial wisdom orientation, then was expanded to have Jesus speak in apocalyptic terms.

The central feature of Q, Koester writes, "was the waiting for the coming of Jesus as the Son of Man (Luke 17:22–37). This expectation, which seems to be missing in the oldest stages of the Synoptic sayings of Jesus, is derived from Jewish apocalyptic concepts (Daniel 7:13–14). In Q it has become the key christological concept for the understanding of Jesus as the redeemer of the future. In contrast, the older expectation of the coming of the rule of God recedes into the background."

Perrin and Koester both feel the apocalyptic "Son of man" sayings were put on Jesus' lips by later believers, but they disagree on the authenticity of many sayings in which Jesus calls for disciples to make radical breaks with family and home life.

Perrin thinks most of them go back to the historical Jesus. But Koester has argued that the early churches' anticipation of the coming Son of man prompted them to invent sayings in which Jesus calls for renunciation of the world and its social bonds. Against Koester, it might be noted that *The Gospel of Thomas* contains some of these radical-break sayings yet no apocalyptic expectation of the Son of man.

The principal method used by Perrin to identify the distinctive sayings of Jesus is called the *criterion of dissimilarity*—"the earliest form of a saying we can reach may be regarded as authentic if it can be shown to be dissimilar to characteristic emphases both of ancient Judaism and of the early Church." Perrin admits that this method is limited in scope. "By definition it will exclude all teaching in which Jesus may have been at one with Judaism or the early Church at one with him," he writes. "But the brutal fact of the matter is that we have no choice. There is simply no other starting point . . .," he says.

Perrin says a second criterion, *coherence*, permits some sayings from an early stratum of the tradition to be accepted if they are consistent with sayings scoring well on the dissimilarity criterion.

A third criterion, Perrin says, is *multiple attestation*, that is, the appearance of the same basic motifs or specific sayings in independent sources. The discovery of *The Gospel of Thomas* served to strengthen this third measure of likely authenticity.

An illustration of the dissimilarity test is Perrin's analysis of Mark 7:15, in which Jesus denies the legitimacy of Jewish dietary laws. It reads, "There is nothing outside a man which by going into him can defile him, but the things which come out of a man are what defile him." Perrin pronounces it as "certainly authentic." It meets the criterion of dissimilarity in that it is "completely without parallel in either rabbinic or sectarian Judaism" and denies the fundamental Jewish distinction between the sacred and the secular, Perrin says. The saying was known also from Matthew 15:10–20 and now is known in *Thomas* 14, a saying in which Jesus advises followers also not to fast, pray, or give alms.

Some features of the historical Jesus drawn by Perrin and Koester, two of the more influential American scholars on this question, look like this: the historical Jesus did not claim to be the Messiah, the Son of God or the Son of man. He proclaimed the dawning of the kingdom, or rule, of God with often stark statements or deceptively simple parables and aphorisms. Jesus rarely, if ever, described himself. He sympathized with the poor and the unpopular. He shunned fasting and certain other religious conventions.

In the late 1970s, Koester, George MacRae, and Robert W. Funk, a New Testament scholar who then headed Scholars Press, started organizing colleagues into a committee that would pursue the Jesus of history by systematically discussing and voting on all sayings attributed to him. The quest for the historical Jesus in more recent decades has attracted a number of scholars such as Funk who have concentrated on the literary analysis of the parables and aphorisms of Jesus. These studies put into bolder relief the literary creativeness—rather than historical memory—that pervades the New Testament Gospels. Literary analysts thus complemented the work of scholars who focused on evidence for sources, editing changes, theological conflicts, and historical settings.

The group met at least once. However, Funk, the key organizer, underwent heart surgery and for various reasons the project was abandoned, or so it seemed.

18. The Jesus Seminar

At Saint Meinrad Archabbey and Seminary, set in the gently rolling hills of southern Indiana, thirty biblical scholars passed a ballot box around the table and dropped colored beads into it: red for yes, pink for maybe, gray for probably not, and black for no.

They were voting on which sayings in the Sermon on the Mount probably go back to Jesus himself and which were placed on his lips by Gospel writers or church tradition. The scholars were to base their votes on the weight of previous critical scholarship, their own research, and whatever insights surfaced in the group's discussions.

Blackballed with virtually no debate was one of Christendom's favorite Beatitudes, or statements of happiness: "Blessed are the peacemakers, for they shall be called sons of God." Similarly, "Blessed are the meek, for they shall inherit the earth" got only six red and pink votes of the thirty cast.

Only three of a dozen "blessings" and "woes" in the Gospels of Matthew and luke were deemed to have derived from Jesus, and a fourth ("blessed are you when men hate you . . .") produced an even split after some debate. Winning favor were the first three Beatitudes as found in Luke 6:20–21—"Blessed are you poor . . . you that hunger . . . you that weep." Also receiving a majority of red votes was *The Gospel of Thomas* version of the first Beatitude—"Blessed are the poor, for yours is the kingdom of heaven" (*Thomas* 54). Scholars also thought that the historical Jesus probably did advise followers to "turn the other cheek" if they met with violence (Matt. 5:39; Luke 6:29).

The discussions and balloting took place at the Roman Catholic seminary on October 11–13, 1985. Following an organizational meeting several months before, the autumn session marked the revival by Robert Funk, with a new set of colleagues, of the effort to seek a consensus on the teachings of the historical Jesus.

George MacRae died that year and Helmut Koester decided not to participate this time. James Robinson took part in the Saint Meinrad meeting, but, like many scholars, he was interested in the group's progress yet found it difficult to invest that much time. Semiannual meetings were expected to continue several years until the approximately five hundred sayings of Jesus were assessed. For the most part, the pool of over a hundred participants represented a younger generation of New Testament scholars active in the field. To be sure, there were other scholars in historical-critical studies who were simply not interested, believing that the historical Jesus is unreachable or that the vote-casting method was unscholarly and ill-conceived.

The rationale for resurrecting the Jesus Seminar, as it was now dubbed, had broadened beyond the aims of scholarship. Mainline Protestant and Catholic churches had never been prone to reveal potentially disturbing biblical research findings in church settings. Moreover, many clergy have been content to think that the historical Jesus is well represented in the New Testament. But in the 1980s charismatic television preachers and prosperous evangelical churches presented to growing audiences a socially and theologically conservative Jesus from a Bible said to be inerrant. It was a challenge unmet by mainline pastors and denominational leaders.

"The religious establishment has not allowed the intelligence of high scholarship to pass through pastors and priests to a hungry laity," Funk said to colleagues at the seminar's organizational meeting in Berkeley. "And the radio and TV counterparts of educated clergy have traded in platitudes and pieties and played on the ignorance of the uninformed."

Part of the blame belonged to scholars, Funk said. New Testament scholars "have not fulfilled their obligations to report their work to a broader public." They "have limited their pronouncements to the classroom or buried their considered judgments in scientific journals and technical jargon." They have hesitated to explain their results in lay terms "out of fear of public controversy and political reprisal."

Another fear many scholars share is the accusation from academic peers that by popularizing (or, more pejoratively, "sensationalizing") their work, they are oversimplifying it and thus distorting scholarship. Most Jesus Seminar members appeared to take those risks in stride. The twice-a-year meetings were open to press coverage.

Participants were aware that what they were probing is sacred to millions. To some faithful, "we will constantly border on blasphemy," Funk said. The reaction, however, proved to be more skeptical than hostile in the first years of the Jesus Seminar.

A widely read religious newspaper in the United Methodist church criticized the project in an editorial. Mistakenly thinking that the Jesus Seminar was attempting to determine the exact words of Jesus rather than his "voice," the style and substance of his teaching, the *United Methodist Reporter* said the New Testament itself is more trustworthy than either scholars or TV evangelists "because it has lasted so long." The Jesus Seminar was "likely to splinter Christians in unhealthy debate," the editorial said.

In a published reply, Hal Taussig, pastor of a Methodist church in Philadelphia and a seminar member, said that "straight and informed talk about the founder of our faith" is healthy. Otherwise, the alternative amounts to a conspiracy "to hide the questions and contradictions." A careful comparison of the biblical Gospels and related texts reveals different Jesuses. "So the reason to consult the biblical scholars is precisely because the New Testament witness is inconsistent," Taussig said.

"Our motives are not to be destructive of faith, nor does anyone think we could be," said seminar member Karen King in an interview. "But scholars do not want to sacrifice intellectual integrity for a naive approach to the texts." In another interview, Yale's Bruce Chilton, who was not a member of the Jesus Seminar, said that mainstream scholars should "come clean" about their views that much of what Jesus says in the Gospels was created after his lifetime. "Basically," Chilton said, "the difference is between an authoritative New Testament or an authoritative Jesus—you can't have them both."

John Dominic Crossan of DePaul University, an influential member of the Jesus Seminar, said at the Saint Meinrad meeting that he seeks to understand "what must have been done and said [by Jesus] to generate such immediate diversity of interpretation."

Depending on which text one uses, Crossan said in a paper prepared for the Saint Meinrad session, "it is possible to reconstruct almost any picture of Jesus one wishes." Jesus can be shown "to be for or against legal observance, for or against apocalyptic expectation, for or against Gentile mission, for or against Temple worship, for or against titular acclaim, for or against political revolt, and so on." As a result, Crossan asked his colleagues to consider the idea that Jesus characteristically said many things that allowed for diverse understanding. Rather than call many Jesus teachings "cryptic," however, Crossan preferred the term "profoundly paradoxical."

The Beatitudes in Matthew's Sermon on the Mount and Luke's Sermon on the Plain lent themselves to various interpretations. When Jesus said, "Blessed are you poor," did he mean the literally poor or "the poor in spirit," as Matthew writes it? Whereas Luke's version was voted "red," Matthew's words "in spirit" received a pink judgment in the initial voting by the Jesus Seminar. Pink meant "Jesus probably said something like this." But red and pink votes were lumped together when determining which sayings would be included in the "data base" of authentic sayings. Organizers reconsidered votes on some tough sayings at later meetings.

Little discussion was needed on the four "woes" in Luke— "woe to the rich, the satiated," and so forth. Most studies have termed them Luke's created counterpoints to "blessed are the poor, the hungry," and so on. For instance, Catholic scholar Joseph Fitzmyer, who was not involved in the Jesus Seminar, says in his Anchor Bible commentary on Luke that the woe sayings in Luke are replete with that author's vocabulary—thus indicating they are his creations.

Some statements of blessedness in Matthew were also thought to be the products of that Gospel author or the church tradition before him. In this case, Old Testament language was thought to be the inspiration. Matthew's Beatitude about the meek inheriting the earth echoes Psalm 37:11, scholars said. Likewise, "Blessed are the pure in heart, for they shall see God," may have been inspired by Psalm 24:3–4.

At the second voting meeting, held at the University of Redlands (California), the seminar deemed as authentic roughly half of thirty-three parables, the form of teaching usually considered the "bedrock" of the Jesus teachings. If a simple majority had been the guideline, then twenty-one of twenty-seven New Testament parables would have gotten the nod and one of six apocryphal parables would have been approved.

The mere consideration of six parables found only in apocryphal writings—namely, three each from *The Gospel of Thomas* and *The Apocryphon of James*—marked a significant step in Jesus research. Charles Hedrick, a veteran of Nag Hammadi studies, had asked fellow seminar members in a straw vote at Saint Meinrad how many people felt *Thomas* was, in effect, simply a rewrite of the canonical Gospels (and thereby of minimal value for their purposes). No one raised a hand.

At Redlands, one *Thomas* parable unparalleled in the synoptic tradition, the "assassin" (*Thomas* 98), was favored by a 16–13 vote. *Thomas* 97, a parable about the woman who discovers that meal spilled out of her cracked jar went down on a 11–18 vote. However, after further discussion at later meetings, seminar fellows found they could not develop a consensus on "the assassin," but eventually gave "the empty jar" a pink vote.

Most remarkable, high marks were given to the *Thomas* versions of parables already known from the biblical gospels. Of nine New Testament parables thought to be authentic, the seminar voted the *Thomas* version closest to the original story in six cases, some narrowly so and some by large margins. One was *Thomas* 64, the dinner guest story, found by Perrin and others to lack the allegorical additions seen in Matthew and Luke. The comparison of the kingdom to the mustard seed (*Thomas* 20) and to the merchant who found a pearl (*Thomas* 76) scored highest; also, the sower (9), the rich farmer (63), and the wicked tenant farmers (64). In fact, the latter parable as told in Mark, Matthew, and Luke were rejected.

Besides voting on individual sayings, the Jesus Seminar assessed various theories about Jesus himself. One long-held scholarly assumption about Jesus "collapsed" at the third Jesus Seminar, held at Notre Dame in October 1986.

Despite the arguments advanced by Koester and Perrin, among others, that the historical Jesus did not preach an apocalyptic message anticipating the imminent end of the world, most scholars assumed that view of Jesus as doomsayer still prevailed. German scholar Albert Schweitzer, prior to his renowned career as a medical missionary in Africa, popularized in 1906 the idea that Jesus taught that the "kingdom of God" pertained to God's dramatic intervention in history within his own generation. But asked if they believed that Jesus did preach an imminent end, only nine of thirty-nine scholars polled by the Jesus Seminar said yes.

"I was frankly surprised at the shift," Funk said, "because most books still present Schweitzer's view." Furthermore, discussions and voting at the Notre Dame meeting made it plain that most seminar members doubted that Jesus predicted the end of the world to occur at any time in the future.

Strong doubts were thus cast on Jesus' references to a divine intervention overthrowing the forces of evil in his generation, such as in Mark 9:11: "Truly, I say to you, there are some standing here who will not taste death before they see the kingdom of God come with power."

The first vote on Mark 9:1 showed an almost even division— thirteen thinking that it was authentic or probably authentic and fourteen thinking not. After debate, the final vote was nine for authenticity and sixteen doubting it. (Vote totals varied because some scholars left before the meeting ended.)

A contradiction had to be settled. The proclamations that the kingdom is in the future belie the Jesus saying that the kingdom had already arrived: "The kingdom of God is not coming with signs to be observed; nor will they say, 'Lo, here it is!' or 'There!' for behold, the kingdom of God is in the midst of you." The initial vote on that passage, Luke 17:20–21, favored its authenticity fifteen to twelve; the final ballot shifted further in its favor, eighteen to seven. *Thomas* 3 and 113 contain similar wording, but did not score as well as the version in Luke.

Among other kingdom sayings affirmed as probably authentic were, "If it is by the finger of God that I cast out demons, then the kingdom of God has come" (Luke 11:20) and "It is easier for a camel to go through the eye of a needle than for a rich man to enter the kingdom of God" (Matt. 19:24).

In spring 1987, the Jesus Seminar voted on the sayings attributed to Jesus in the Passion and resurrection accounts. All of them, including Jesus' predictions of his own death and the "seven last words" from the cross, were seen as the product of the early church's reflection about the crucifixion. Many critical studies had already come to that conclusion or had proceeded on that assumption, but it was rarely said to the general public.

The words of Jesus on the cross are largely quotations from or allusions to Jewish Scriptures, which were called upon to interpret the significance of Jesus' death, said seminar member Marcus Borg of Oregon State University. "It's not impossible at all to believe that Jesus might have prayed a prayer from the Old Testament while dying on the cross," Borg said. "But it's very difficult to believe that, on the cross, he was interpreting the meaning of his own death by quoting Scripture."

The Jesus Seminar indicated that little was historically sure about Jesus' last days other than he was crucified in Jerusalem around Passover during the Roman rule of Pontius Pilate. In a statement adopted almost unanimously and important for Jewish-Christian relations, the seminar said: "There was no Jewish trial of Jesus before the Roman authority executed him, and there was no Jewish crowd involved in his condemnation." A number of Christian churches, desiring to correct past wrongs, have declared in recent years that there is no continuing Jewish responsibility for Jesus' death. But, as one seminar member noted, "the Jesus Seminar affirmed that there was no such responsibility in the first place."

The voting results reported here should be considered unofficial yet reflecting the direction of the debates. This writer attended the first three meetings and reported on them for the *Los Angeles Times*. Official results and many of the papers presented for the meetings are published in *Foundations & Facets Forum*, edited by Funk at his Polebridge Press in Sonoma, California.

As the list of unexamined Jesus sayings grew smaller, the Jesus Seminar continued to treat Mark, Matthew, Luke, and *Thomas* as its primary sources. In October 1987 gathering at Luther-Northwestern Seminary in St. Paul, Minnesota, *Thomas* 86 about the "foxes have holes" and its equivalents in Matthew and Luke received favor, as did *Thomas* 78 ("into the desert") and the canonical parallels.

One Jesus saying, about washing the outside of the cup, would perhaps not have been regarded authentic except for the untainted version in *Thomas*. Its equivalents in Matthew (23:25–26) and Luke (11:39–41) have Jesus addressing an admonition in angry tones to the Pharisees, who some scholars tend to think were opponents of the early church but not necessarily of Jesus. Here is the *Thomas* version:

(89) Jesus said, "Why do you wash the outside of the cup? Do you not realize that he who made the inside is the same one who made the outside?"

This seems to be one of those cryptic sayings that Crossan would say lends itself to varied interpretations.

A recurring issue was whether seminar scholars were being guided in their voting by how the sayings fit their own image of the historical Jesus. Members frequently said they struggled to put their preconceptions aside and consider each saying on its own merits and in the context of related sayings.

Burton Mack, a professor at the School of Theology at Claremont, said that his research led him to believe that Jesus was primarily a purveyor of wisdom and aphorisms. Though Jewish, Jesus resembled the Cynic philosopher of the pervasive first-century Greek culture more than he did a Jewish prophet, in Mack's view, also expressed in his 1988 book *The Myth of Innocence*. Jesus' authentic sayings show "a playfulness, exuberance and cleverness typical of Hellenistic philosophers who were critical of social conventions and seeking a free and iconoclastic style of life," Mack suggested during one of the seminar meetings.

In reply, Dennis R. MacDonald, another seminary teacher who was then a visiting professor at Harvard Divinity School, said that if Mack's picture of a benign Jesus is true, "then the Romans made a bigger mistake [in crucifying Jesus] than I thought they did."

Ron Cameron then startled his colleagues: "The death of Jesus was like a car wreck; it was an accident of history." Later, Cameron said, "I'm not sure why the Romans killed Jesus, but the Gospel stories are not historical in the modern sense of the word.

"I don't take the death of Jesus as unimportant," said Cameron, of Wesleyan University in Middleton, Connecticut. "But loading it with Christian theological freight, as is generally done by Christians, of which I am one, strikes me as bad theology. I don't think Jesus had the notoriety that the Gospels say he had. His [authentic] sayings don't anywhere give evidence that he was trying to found a church or a reform movement."

At the Notre Dame meeting, John L. White of Loyola University of Chicago said two "mutually exclusive" models of Jesus seemed to be at work behind much of the voting. One was the image emphasized by Mack and Cameron—that Jesus was raised in Galilee in a quasi-Gentile setting, taught a Hellenistic form of wisdom despite tensions with institutional Judaism, and that if any political or religious objections to Jesus actually arose, they were ill-founded.

The other model of Jesus was a more Jewish one—closer to one defined by Borg. This second model, broadly speaking, held that Jesus was raised in Galilee in a Jewish setting and he advocated "a new order comprehensible to a Jewish audience," much like a Jewish prophet, White said. Subsequently, Jesus came into conflict with the existing religious and political order, which "led directly and deliberately to his execution."

The Jesus Seminar, its work incomplete as this book went to press, was not expected to be the last word on the historical Jesus. Yet it moved the debate along at a greater speed than the usual pace of scholarship. It also challenged scholars and clergy alike to be more honest and frank. However tentative the final pictures of Jesus might be, there was a growing amount of substantial evidence showing what he did *not* claim to be and what he did *not* say.

The discovery of the Nag Hammadi library—most of all, the discovery of Codex II, tractate 2—contributed greatly to this vigorous new search. The content of *The Gospel of Thomas* reinforced some suspicions already gaining strength in studies of the canonical Gospels. The Jesus of myth and pure invention was proving to be pervasive in the New Testament Gospels. The Nag Hammadi library gave the world more details about the Jesus of heresy, but it also provided valuable clues to the Jesus of history.

19. The Judas Puzzle

The Gospel of Thomas has been unanimously regarded by scholars as a random collection of sayings with no rhyme or reason in its sequence—as improbable as that seems. *Thomas* lacks continuity, as "familiar sayings appear in . . . unfamiliar groupings," said Robert M. Wilson in the mid-1960s. The sayings are "unconnected and in no particular order," wrote Bentley Layton in 1987.

Catchword associations sometimes link sayings, such as in *Thomas* 73, 74, and 75. But that kind of word linkage "represents the most minimal form of composition," wrote John Dominic Crossan.

Stevan L. Davies attempted to divide *Thomas* into four sections bearing recurring themes. However, rarely does a motif repeat in all four of his sections. He admitted that if the ordering was intentional, the reasoning escaped him. "I look forward to the time when someone unambiguously uncovers the secret to *Thomas*'s order or, indeed, to the time when we can conclude that the sayings are essentially random . . .," Davies wrote in his 1983 book on *Thomas*.

The "secret," I believe, lies in the realization that *The Gospel of Thomas* was once purposely arranged but that the pattern was obscured when changes were made in the text. New sayings were inserted, and existing sayings were often moved or combined. I suggested in Chapter 17 that the first version was attributed simply to Judas (without the name Thomas) and sayings 12, 13, and 114 were added as well. But these were only a few of the additions.

The solution to the order in *Thomas* eluded scholars because they nearly always treated the text as essentially the work of one author. Davies did too, except for 114, which he felt contained ideas and vocabulary foreign to the rest of the text. If 114 was appended, however, that means that sayings 3 and 113, which have an identical theme, open and close the collection. (*Thomas* 1 and 2 are introductory sayings.) When Davies mentioned that to me in a phone conversation, it made me think that a pattern might emerge if many other sayings of dubious origin were ignored.

I must speak personally now of my own research. I found that sayings were once elegantly arranged before they were jumbled. Offered here is a refined version of my findings presented at the 1985 Pacific Coast meeting of the Society of Biblical Literature. My "solution" remains the same: ninety-three sayings arranged into intricate series according to format and/or subject matters. Reconstructing the original text with full confidence may await further studies, but I believe the framework of the puzzle is now exposed.

At the very least, it is clear that *The Gospel of Thomas* should no longer be treated as the work of one author. Certainly, no one doubts that *Thomas* underwent some editing in its history. That is obvious from comparisons of the Coptic text with the three Greek fragments of *Thomas* found around the turn of this century at Oxyrhynchus, Egypt:

—Papyrus Oxyrhynchus 654 (POxy 654): The main difference is in the prologue in which the writer is identified as "[Judas, who is] also Thomas" rather than "Didymos Judas Thomas." *Thomas* 2 in POxy 654 invites the reader to "seek, find, be amazed, rule and rest," but the Coptic says seek, find, become troubled, be astonished, and rule over the all. The Greek rendition seems older than the Coptic version.

—Papyrus Oxyrhynchus 1 (POxy 1): The biggest disparity in these sayings, from 26 through 33, is the presence of a saying attached to the end of *Thomas* 77 in the Coptic text. In the Greek text, it reads, "Lift up the stone, and you will find me there. Split the piece of wood, and I am there." In the Greek fragment it appears at the end of *Thomas* 30.

—Papyrus Oxyrhynchus 655 (POxy 655): This has a much wordier, perhaps a later, version of *Thomas* 36, which in the Coptic text has Jesus advising against worrying day and night about what to wear.

The Gospel of Thomas has one striking alteration that must have occurred fairly early in the text's history; the change is seen in both the Coptic and POxy 654 versions. It pertains to the disciples' question about prayer, fasting, and almsgiving—three pillars of piety in Jewish antiquity—and whether certain foods should be avoided. As it now stands, the question is in *Thomas* 6 and the answer is in *Thomas* 14:

(6) His disciples questioned him and said to him, "Do you want us to fast? How shall we pray? Shall we give alms? What diet shall be observe?"

Jesus said, "Do not tell lies, and do not do what you hate, for all things are plain in the sight of heaven."

"For nothing hidden will not become manifest, and nothing covered will remain without being uncovered."

(14) Jesus said to them, "If you feast, you will give rise to sin for yourselves; and if you pray, you will be condemned; and if you give alms, you will do harm to your spirits. When you go into any land and walk about the districts, if they receive you, eat what they will set before you, and heal the sick among you.

"For what goes into your mouth will not defile you, but that which issues from your mouth—it is that which will defile you."

Jesus' response to the four questions in 6—"do not tell lies, and do not do what you hate"—is a conceivable answer, yet it is really unsatisfactory. By comparison, in 14 the four questions are answered specifically and in the same order.

And, decisively, 14 is the lone saying in *Thomas* that begins, "Jesus said to them." In a dozen other sayings with the wording "Jesus [or he] said to them," Jesus is replying to a question or statement (see, for example, 12, 20, 22, 51, 52, 53, 79, 91)!

The Gospel of Thomas continued to undergo changes beyond those visible in the Greek and Coptic versions now available. The early third-century church father Hippolytus said the Naassene Gnostics used a *Gospel According to Thomas* in which it said, "He who seeks will find me in children from seven years onwards; for there I am found, who am hidden, in the fourteenth aeon." This sounds like a distorted conflation of *Thomas* 2 ("seek and find") and 4, which talks about "a small child seven days old" who is wiser than old men. (*Thomas* 4 strikes some as sectarian creation, but the imagery bears a strong affinity to Luke 10:21 and Matthew 11:25, in which Jesus thanks God for hiding things from the supposedly wise and revealing them to "babes," a likely codeword for disciples.)

Initial studies of *Thomas* could not help but notice other terms and ideas used by the Naassenes, as reported by Hippolytus. The similarities led William R. Schoedel in 1960 to say cautiously that the evidence lends support to the hypothesis that *Thomas* was either composed or thoroughly edited by the Naassene sect. Yet it is also possible that the Naassene sect was an outgrowth or a descendant of the group that made the peculiar additions to *Thomas*.

Schoedel at least recognized the possibility that the *Gospel of Thomas* might have undergone a thorough editing. Granting that *Thomas can* be read presently as a Gnostic document, Wilson nevertheless asked whether "a document originally non-Gnostic has been taken over, adapted and embellished to serve a Gnostic purpose." Years later, Marvin W. Meyer characterized the writing as one "edited and revised by Christians with gnosticizing interests."

In a limited concession to that possibility, Koester said sayings 83–85 may be "later interpolations" into *Thomas*. "A few sayings in *The Gospel of Thomas* reveal the influence of speculations about the biblical creation story (redemption as the rediscovery of the heavenly prototypes that are superior to the earthly Adam)," Koester wrote in his *Introduction to the New Testament*.

Indeed, *Thomas* 84 has Jesus say in part, "When you see your images which came into being before you, and which neither die nor become manifest, how much you will have to bear!" One's primordial image and origin in the heavenly light is also the theme in 83 and 50. *Thomas* 19 says in part, "Blessed is he who came into being before he came into being." A great number of these sayings can be associated by motif and vocabulary (see Appendix).

The problem, of course, is where to stop. Some terms and motifs were shared by many religious movements. And undeniably this overlap in expression makes it hard to draw the line between added and original material.

My working assumption was that the compiler used sayings typical of those found in the synoptic Gospels and in non-Gnostic apocryphal works with affinities to *Thomas*. In taking those guidelines I saw ground rules emerge for an underlying puzzle very different from and much more elaborate than the biblical chiasm, the playful concentric arrangement of words and sentences commonly employed by both Old and New Testament writers.

It seems certain that the compiler placed sayings in varying patterns and sequences into the first and second halves, the middle saying being *Thomas* 53. As the text exists now, that saying is not the midpoint—there are 114 sayings in the collection, not 106. But certain types of sayings tended to fall before or after 53. For instance, sayings referring to the disciples as children occur only in the first half: 4, 21a, 22, 37, 46, and 50. (Later, I argue that 50 is an insert and 37 belongs in another series.) Sayings about a new understanding of mother, father, and family are in the second half: 55, 99, 101, and 105. Synopticlike beatitudes—"blessed is . . ."—all occur in the second half: 54, 58, 68, 69, 79, and 103. The one "woe" (102, "to the Pharisees") also appears in the second half. Four beatitudes are seen in the first half, but they bear the distinctive Gnostic-like, or sectarian, themes of discovering one's origins (18b, 19, and 49) or consuming the dead (7), a strange theme used also in 11b and 60.

Parables show up primarily in the second half. In this instance, the placement is asymmetrical. With only a modest amount of reconstruction, we can see four groups containing three each in the second half and one group of three in the first half. Two such clusters of three consecutive parables (63–64–65 and 96–97–98) had already been noticed by scholars. But if we assume that the text originally grouped other parables and extended pronouncements in groups of three, then we can postulate two other second-half groupings:

1. *Thomas* 76, a parable comparing the kingdom to a merchant who found a pearl, would form a trio with 78 and 79 were it not for saying 77, which has Jesus describe himself as "the light" and "the all." Nos. 78 and 79 are not parables by modern reckoning but they appear to function like such stories in this sayings collection.

2. The kingdom is compared to certain men in 107 and 109 and also in the only parable left in the second half, 57. I believe that all three were originally together.

The motive for this latter shift—as well as all moves by the principal editor—is to place sayings containing an identical word (or motif) next to each other. *Thomas* 108 was moved to that position because it says the "hidden" will be revealed. The next saying, *Thomas* 109, is a parable about "hidden" treasure. In removing the parable about a "man" from the place between 107 and 109, the editor put it before one of his insertions, 58, which has Jesus say, "Blessed is the *man* who has suffered and found *life*." Saying 58, in turn, was linked with catchwords in 59, an original saying in which Jesus admonishes, "Take heed of the *living* one while you are *alive* . . ." (italics mine).

Three parables appear in the first half. Together are 8 and 9, parables about a wise fisherman and the sower, respectively. The other parable is *Thomas* 20, about the mustard seed. It is conceivable that 20 once formed a trio with 8 and 9 because of similar groupings in the second half. Why was 20 moved? Again, the only reason seems to be the editor's desire to create catchword associations from one saying to another, especially when he inserts a new saying. In this case, 19 speaks of "the five trees in paradise"; 20 describes the mustard seed that "produces a great plant." Perhaps to continue the theme, the next saying is 21, which talks about little children who settle in a field not theirs.

Another asymmetrical arrangement is used for sayings about the "hidden to be disclosed" or "the select number who will learn the mysteries," to paraphrase them. They occur once in the first half (5) and four times in the second half (62, 75, 94, and 108). In two cases (62 and 75), they sit right before a trio of parables. In the other instances, they could have once been in that position. Some explanations are needed here to say why these particular five form a series:

I omitted, for example, 6b, which thrice states that everything shall be revealed. The very repetition indicates an editor's elaboration, but, more than that, the main point of 6b is an admonition by Jesus not to lie or do what you hate.

I included 75 despite its sectarian tone. It says, "Many are standing at the door, but it is the solitary who will enter the bridal chamber." My guess is that *Thomas* 75 once said something like many are standing at the door but "few" will enter. That would be consistent with a Jesus saying in Matthew 22:14—"For many are called, but few are chosen."

The word "solitary," as we shall see, designates the sectarian believer. In *Thomas* 49, the term is part of a saying added to the original text. But in 75 and 16 I think the word "solitary" is inserted into an original saying. It makes sense that an editor would feel free to alter some words in the compiler's collection as well as to insert whole new sayings. As a result, we should not automatically discard a whole saying as secondary when it contains some of an editor's jargon. But it must fit into a thematic or format series and be consistent with other early Jesus material to be considered a saying in the original collection.

Were it not for those guidelines, the overly elaborate *Thomas* 22 might be seen as an addition. It was heavily expanded by an editor, but its core idea of the two becoming one, neither male nor female, is attested elsewhere in early Jesus circles.

The "bridal chamber" in 75 (and 104) presents a different problem. Although it is a sacrament in *The Gospel of Philip* and other Gnostic lore, the ritual reunification of the sexes is implied in the idea of "the two shall become one." So we cannot immediately rule out the possibility of an early wing of the Jesus movement using the "bridal chamber" in such rites. As such, it would be a ceremony where secrets are revealed—making 75 an apt saying in the sequence of "the hidden to be revealed to the few." Another such saying, 94, has Jesus say, "He who seeks will find, and [he who knocks] will be let in." That is consistent with the image of those who stand at the door and who wish to enter (75).

However, if an otherwise credible saying breaks up a well-established pattern, it is suspect as an addition. Such is the trouble with 95, Jesus's admonition to give money without interest to those who will not give it back, an idea with synoptic parallels. *Thomas* 95 separates 94 from the parable trio of 96–97–98 and it cannot be linked with another series.

With most parables and their antecedent mystery-revealing sayings located in the second half, the imbalance must be righted. The answer lies partly in the placement of proverbs in the first half, ten in all. One uninterrupted string extends from 31 ("No prophet is accepted in his own village . . .") to 35.

These are the relatively visible signs of organization in the present copies of *The Gospel of Thomas*. Obviously, more must be known about the editors in order to complete the story of the puzzle and the surprise it has.

Actually, the Judas sayings collection was subjected to at least two distinct stages of editing. The respective changes are indicated in the text found in the Appendix.

The first editor did the most damage. He was the one I described for the most part. His recurring vocabulary is noted in the margins. This editor probably renamed the sayings collection *The Gospel of Thomas* and added the name Thomas to Judas in the prologue. He inserts and reassembles sayings according to catchword association or related motifs, supposedly to enhance "interpretation," or so the intent seemed to be. Saying 1 is this editor's introductory saying. Fellow believers are the "solitary" and "the elect." Another expression for believers, "the single one," literally, "the one and the same," may have been used by both editors.

The second editor, whose work is not evident in POxy 654, has Jesus talk about "the all." The additions betray an appreciative knowledge of the Gospel of John, adding "Didymos" to the names Judas and Thomas in the prologue, for instance. Like John, this editor has Jesus explain his divine nature. Catchword associations are rarely used.

About one-fourth of *The Gospel of Thomas*, as seen in the Nag Hammadi library, consists of editorial additions. I have identified twenty-five whole sayings inserted into the original collection (1, 7, 12, 13, 19, 24, 29, 30, 43, 49, 50, 56, 58, 60, 67, 74, 80, 83, 84, 85, 87, 95, 100, 112, and 114). Substantial additions were made to eleven sayings (3, 11, 18, 22, 43, 61, 64, 68, 69, 77, and 111). And four sayings that apparently stood alone in the original compilation were attached to other original sayings (14b, 21b, 21c, and 22b).

Were any sayings in the first version of the text deleted? My proposed solution to the puzzle tells me no.

Starting at the dividing point in the collection, what is now *Thomas* 53 but was the 47th saying in the original, the reader would see Jesus answering the disciples' question about circumcision. It forms a series with two other sayings having the same narrative format and the same negative response about Jewish religious law—the once-together 6a–14a (questions and answers about fasting, praying, almsgiving, and diet) and 104 (Jesus' upset answer when "they" urge him to join in prayer and fasting). By eliminating inserted sayings from consideration and allowing for shuffling by the editor of original sayings, we could locate 6a–14a as saying no. 10. That would match 104's position ten places from the last original saying, 113. (I omit 112 as an insertion but I moved 57 "back" to form a trio with fellow parables 107 and 109.) Saying 27, which redefines fasting and the Sabbath, can be ruled out as a fourth saying in this series because it does not have Jesus responding to a question or statement.

The question-and-answer format also helps to identify another series. Sayings 18, 22b, 37, 51, and 91 each depict the disciples eager to know things that Jesus says is available to them now. His answers are sometimes similar to the opening and closing themes—3a and 113. These "moment is now" sayings form an asymmetrical pattern: four in the first half and one in the second half.

It was tempting to see 37 not as a "moment is now" saying but as more suited to a "secret wisdom" sequence, to be discussed next. I had to choose, because I determined that no saying served more than one sequence. Jesus' answer in 37 fits the secret wisdom series, but the disciples' question signals the "seeking" readers that the "moment is now" is the correct category.

Perhaps the most meaningful sequence of sayings for the compiler—even more than those combatting apocalyptic speculation in 3, 18, 51, and 113—was the "secret wisdom" pattern. Interlocking with that sequence are two series already mentioned: sayings about children entering the kingdom in the first half and Jesus' words about the new understanding of parents in the second half. These esoteric sayings form a larger pattern with eight "secret wisdom" sayings (four in each half) about "the heavens passing away," seeing "the living one" or "the father," and making the two into one.

Here is the pattern:
Disciples enter as children / New understanding of parents

4   21a   22   46   55   99   101   105

Secret wisdom: heavens . . . seeing divine . . . make two into one

11a   15   48   52   59   61a   106   111a

The placement of these sixteen sayings was especially intricate. *Thomas* 4 is the first saying after the opening theme (3a) and 111a is the last saying before the closing saying (113), since 112 is an identifiable addition to the text. As previously argued, 53 marks the middle of the document. Saying 52 is the last saying of the first half and 55 is supposed to be the first saying of the second half. *Thomas* 54 ("Blessed are the poor . . .") could very well have been switched with 55 in order for the latter saying, which starts off, "Whoever . . .", to link up with 56, which starts the same way.

The sayings about children, parents, and secret wisdom include what could be called "doublets," sayings that are variations of essentially the same saying. Compare 11a and 111a about the heavens rolling away, 48 and 106 about the two becoming one and able to move mountains, and 55 and 101 about hating one's mother and father in order to become Jesus' disciple. On recognizing the compiler's intentions, we can see the reason for the duplicate sayings: they are needed to fill out the balanced patterns.

These surely are deliberate attempts to give the reader in antiquity something to seek, find, and be amazed at—as promised in saying 2. Ideas most important to the compiler are placed at the start, middle, and conclusion, and a consistency emerges. By contrast, the editors' sayings do not form discernible patterns of their own, nor do they join up with the compiler's sayings.

Can the reader who finds these ideas positioned in puzzle patterns think the author would stop there? Doesn't logic compel one to look for every saying to have its proper place? That was my thinking. To make it work, I have to count some sayings that read a bit like those I have called editorial insertions. Two are sayings in which Jesus speaks with the voice of Wisdom in Gnostic-like terms (28 and 30b). Another two have Jesus say that those who become rich should renounce power or the world (81 and 110). Despising the world is a theme of the first editor, but becoming "rich" (in wisdom) can be defended as characteristic of the compiler's theology.

It may be felt that my method of reconstruction takes too many liberties in moving sayings to new positions. Yet, if the puzzle accommodates every saying, and if every saying belongs to a definite pattern, and if most patterns interlock with a second one, the possibilities for manipulation are limited.

For this chart I have put new numbers for the original sequence of sayings into boxes below the numbers now used in *The Gospel of Thomas*. The prologue originally read: "These are the secret sayings which the living Jesus spoke and which Judas wrote down."

- Introductory saying to "seek, find, be amazed, rule and rest."

2
┌───┐
│ 1 │
└───┘

- Identical theme opens and closes collection—that the kingdom is in and around us and present now.

3 and 113
┌───┐   ┌────┐
│ 2 │   │ 93 │
└───┘   └────┘

- Question or exhortation about Jewish religious customs and negative replies (No. 47 separated the halves.)

6a–14a   53   104
┌────┐   ┌────┐   ┌────┐
│ 10 │   │ 47 │   │ 84 │
└────┘   └────┘   └────┘

- I cast fire and disruption but I bring rest for you.

disruption   assurance   disruption   assurance

10   16   23   71   82   90
┌────┐ ┌────┐ ┌────┐   ┌────┐   ┌────┐ ┌────┐
│ 8 │ │ 13 │ │ 19 │   │ 60 │   │ 68 │ │ 72 │
└────┘ └────┘ └────┘   └────┘   └────┘ └────┘

Admonitions on behavior and encouragement on inner strength.

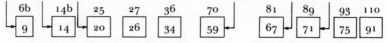

6b   14b   25   27   36   70   81   89   93   110
┌────┐ ┌────┐ ┌────┐ ┌────┐ ┌────┐ ┌────┐   ┌────┐ ┌────┐ ┌────┐ ┌────┐
│ 9 │ │ 14 │ │ 20 │ │ 26 │ │ 34 │ │ 59 │   │ 67 │ │ 71 │ │ 75 │ │ 91 │
└────┘ └────┘ └────┘ └────┘ └────┘ └────┘   └────┘ └────┘ └────┘ └────┘

• Proverbs . . .   / Beatitudes and a woe.

21b/21c/26/45/47   31–35   54   68/69b   102/103
[21–25]   [29–33] [49] [57/58]   [82/83]

• Prophetic statements, admonitions, and other sayings.

39/40/41/42/44   66   72/73   86/88
[37–41]   [50] [61/62] [69/70]

• The hidden to be revealed to selected numbers.

5   62   75   94   108
[4]   [53]   [63]   [76]   [87]

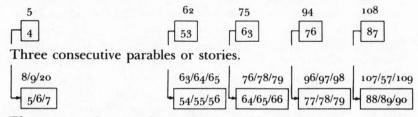

• Three consecutive parables or stories.

8/9/20   63/64/65   76/78/79   96/97/98   107/57/109
[5/6/7]   [54/55/56] [64/65/66] [77/78/79] [88/89/90]

• The moment is now, always opening with a query.

18   22b   37   51   91
[15] [27] [35] [44]   [73]

• Jesus speaks in first person with voice of Wisdom.

17   28   38   30b/77b   92
[16] [28] [36] [45]   [74]

• Disciples enter as children   / New understanding of parents.

4   21a/22a   46   55   99/101   105
[3]   [17/18]   [42] [48]   [80/81] [85]

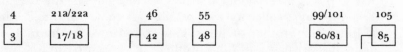

• Secret wisdom: heavens . . . seeing divine . . . make two into one.

11a/15   48   52   59/61a   106   111a
[11/12]   [43] [46] [51/52]   [86] [92]

By identifying such intricate placement as the work of the original author and the catchword associations with the principal editor, we can work toward isolating the traits of an early Jesus movement. The secret wisdom sayings are not Gnostic or Naassene. It would take a whole book to argue the case, but I believe that the formula two shall become one, the babe "seven days old" (*Thomas* 4), and the idea of seeing God go back to the earliest decades after Jesus. If 101 refers to a heavenly mother (the saying is damaged in the Coptic text), then it can be studied in connection with a reference by Jesus in *The Apocryphon of James* to himself as "son of the Holy Spirit" and his speaking of "my mother, the Holy Spirit" in *The Gospel of the Hebrews*.

If the existence of the underlying puzzle is confirmed by further studies, then it becomes possible to date the text's stages of development. The last changes may have been made in the early second century by an editor influenced by the Gospel of John. To repeat my earlier proposal, the principal editor apparently felt the Judas sayings collection was in danger of being discredited in view of the impact of the Gospel of Mark after 70 C.E. According to Mark, Judas the brother of Jesus was not a follower, whereas a Judas Iscariot was the betrayer of Jesus. The editor apparently gave Judas a second name, Thomas, and thus worked the authority figure for the secret sayings back into "the Twelve," as listed by Mark.

The Q sayings source, according to some scholars, was composed around the middle of the first century. The Q document, they say, underwent alterations with the addition of apocalyptic sayings, such as those about the coming Son of man.

It seems reasonable to surmise that the Judas collection was formed with 3a and 113 as bookends to the puzzle by a compiler who was concerned about the lure of apocalyptic thinking. If that step was taken about the time Q was altered, the original "secret sayings" collection was possibly assembled in the lifetime of Judas, the brother of Jesus. Paul complained in the mid-50s about the privileges of "the brothers of the Lord" in 1 Corinthians. Again, available texts indicate James and Judas were the only siblings of Jesus who carried great authority.

The quest for the historical Jesus may have to explore more paths. As open-minded as Jesus Seminar members are to different models of the historical Jesus, they have not seriously entertained the possibility of Jesus as mystagogue, or, to put it less provocatively, Jesus as the teacher of both ordinary and secret wisdom.

Also, the question of whether very early Jesus followers or Jesus himself were influenced by Gnostic ideas should not be ignored. Nag Hammadi studies have shown that the likely beginnings of Gnosticism go back to a period contemporary with Jesus and within Jewish circles. The Sethian Gnostics showed a disdain for the Jewish Creator—something lacking in Jesus's sayings—but the notions of a heavenly father-mother-son triad and rites to facilitate an ascent to the heavens should not be deemed completely foreign to the early Jesus movement.

Finally, the difficulty of reaching the Jesus of history stems from the unavoidable fact that many of Jesus' parables and aphorisms considered authentic seem to be purposely obscure. We probably cannot blame our dim perception entirely on the distance in time and circumstances. Was the intent of Jesus to be playful or profound? Words assembled in the Judas puzzle are both. The puzzle solution points to how becoming children in a new spiritual family is related to other esoteric wisdom apparently attained through sacred rituals. We don't know if the beliefs of the one who assembled the sayings truly represented what Jesus taught, but *The Gospel of Thomas*, as reconstructed, possibly places us closer in time and family relationships to Jesus than ever before. May subsequent, open-eyed research be "worthy" of the mysteries that they may be revealed (*Thomas* 62, 5) and we can attain rest (*Thomas* 2 [POxy 654]).

Appendix: The Altered Text

The Nag Hammadi version of Thomas reprinted here is the revised (1988) translation by Thomas O. Lambdin. The symbol [] indicates missing words in damaged text and ⟨⟩ indicates words omitted long ago in the copying or editing.

The first editor's likeliest additions are *italicized*; the probable insertions by the second editor are <u>underlined</u>. In the right-hand margin are cross-references to words and motifs used by editors—catchwords that account for sayings moved or inserted by the first editor, and wording of the second editor which has parallels in the Gospel of John. (See last chapter for fuller explanation.) Notable variants to Nag Hammadi versions are in footnotes.

These are the secret sayings which the living Jesus spoke and which <u>Didymos</u> Judas *Thomas* wrote down.

Didymos: John 11:16; 20:24; 21:2. Thomas: 13, title.

(1) *And he said, "Whoever finds the interpretation of these sayings will not experience death."*

not experience death: 18, 19, 85.

(2) Jesus said, "Let him who seeks continue seeking until he finds. When he finds, he will become troubled. When he becomes troubled, he will be astonished, and he will rule <u>over the all</u>."

the all: 67, 77.

(3)(a) Jesus said, "If those who lead you say to you, 'See, the kingdom is in the sky,' then the birds of the sky will precede you. If they say to you, 'It is in the sea,' then the fish will precede you. Rather the kingdom is inside of you, and it is outside of you.

(b) *"When you come to know yourselves, then you will become known, and you will realize that it is you*

know/find self: 111b.

Prologue. POxy 654: "These are the [secret] sayings [which] the living Jesus [spoke, and which Judas, *who is*] *also Thomas*, [wrote down]."

2. POxy 654: [Jesus said], "Let him who seeks continue [seeking until] he finds. When he finds, [he will be amazed. And] when he becomes [amazed], he will rule. And [once he has ruled], he will [attain rest]."

2. From *The Gospel of the Hebrews*: "He that seeks will not rest until he finds; and he that has found shall marvel; and he that has marveled shall reign: and he that has reigned shall rest" (source: Clement of Alexandria).

who are the sons of the living father. But if you will *living father: 50.*
not know yourselves, you dwell in poverty and it is
you who are that poverty."
poverty: 29.

(4) Jesus said, "The man old in days will not
hesitate to ask a small child seven days old   place(s): 24, 60, 64,
about *the place of* life, and he will live. For many   68.
who are first will become last, *and they will be-*
come one and the same."
one and the same,
(5) Jesus said, "Recognize what is in your   single one: 22, 23,
sight, and that which is hidden from you will   30 (POxy 1).
become plain to you. For there is nothing hidden which will not become manifest."

(6)(a) His disciples questioned him and said   6a moved here from
to him, "Do you want us to fast? How shall we   start of 14.
pray? Shall we give alms? What diet shall we
observe?"

(b) Jesus said, "Do not tell lies, and do not
do what you hate, for all things are plain in
the sight of heaven. For nothing hidden will
not become manifest, and nothing covered will
remain without being uncovered."

(7) *Jesus said, "Blessed is the lion which becomes*
man when consumed by man; and cursed is the man   eat dead: 11b, 60.
whom the lion consumes, and the lion becomes man."   catchword "man."

(8) And he said, "The man is like a wise fisherman who cast his net into the sea and drew
it up from the sea full of small fish. Among
them the wise fisherman found a fine large
fish. He threw all the small fish back into the
sea and chose the large fish without difficulty.
Whoever has ears to hear, let him hear."

(9) Jesus said, "Now the sower went out, took
a handful (of seeds), and scattered them. Some
fell on the road; the birds came and gathered
them up. Others fell on rock, did not take root
in the soil, and did not produce ears. And
others fell on thorns; they choked the seed(s)

---

6. POxy 654: "[His disciples] questioned him [and said], 'How [shall we] fast?
[How shall we pray]? How [shall we give alms]? What [diet] shall [we] observe?'
Jesus said, '[Do not tell lies, and] do not do what you [hate, for all things are
plain in the sight] of truth. [For nothing] hidden [will not become manifest].' "

and worms ate them. And others fell on the good soil and it produced good fruit: it bore sixty per measure and a hundred and twenty per measure."

(10) Jesus said, "I have cast fire upon the world, and see, I am guarding it until it blazes."

(11)(a) Jesus said, "This heaven will pass away and the one above it will pass away. The dead are not alive, and the living will not die.

(b) *"In the days when you consumed what is dead, you made it what is alive. When you come to dwell in the light, what will you do? On the day when you were one you became two. But when you become two, what will you do?"*

(12) *The disciples said to Jesus, "We know that you will depart from us. Who is to be our leader?"*

Jesus said to them, "Wherever you are, you are to go to James the righteous, for whose sake heaven and earth came into being."

(13) *Jesus said to his disciples, "Compare me to someone and tell me whom I am like."*

Simon Peter said to him, "You are like a righteous angel."

Matthew said to him, "You are like a wise philosopher."

Thomas said to him, "Master, my mouth is wholly incapable of saying whom you are like."

Jesus said, "I am not your master. Because you have drunk, you have become intoxicated from the bubbling spring which I have measured out."

And he took him and withdrew and told him three things. When Thomas returned to his companions, they asked him, "What did Jesus say to you?"

Thomas said to them, "If I tell you one of the things which he told me, you will pick up stones and throw them at me; a fire will come out of the stones and burn you up."

(14)(a) Jesus said to them, "If you fast, you will give rise to sin for yourselves; and if you pray, you will be condemned; and if you give alms, you will do harm to your spirits. When you go into any land and walk about in the

---

catchword "die/dead." eat dead: 7, 60.

catchword "heaven." (death motif?)

Simon Peter: 114.

Thomas: prologue, title.

stones: 19.

Questions moved to 6a; 3 answers follow "3 things" in 13.

districts, if they receive you, eat what they will set before you, and heal the sick among them.

(b) "For what goes into your mouth will not defile you, but that which issues from your mouth—it is that which will defile you."

14b attached due to eating motif.

(15) Jesus said, "When you see one who was not born of woman, prostrate yourselves on your faces and worship him. That one is your father."

(16) Jesus said, "Men think, perhaps, that it is peace which I have come to cast upon the world. They do not know that it is dissension which I have come to cast upon the earth: fire, sword, and war. For there will be five in a house: three will be against two, and two against three, the father against the son, and the son against the father. *And they will stand solitary.*"

solitary: 49, 75.

(17) Jesus said, "I shall give you what no eye has seen and what no ear has heard and what no hand has touched and what has never occurred to the human mind."

(18) The disciples said to Jesus, "Tell us how our end will be."

17 and 18 switched to link disciples in 18, 19, 20, 21, 22, 23, 24.

Jesus said, "Have you discovered, then, the beginning, that you look for the end? For where the beginning is, there will the end be. *Blessed is he who will take his place in the beginning: he will know the end and will not experience death.*"

origin motif: 19, 49, 50, 84.

(19) *Jesus said, "Blessed is he who came into being before he came into being. If you become my disciples and listen to my words, these stones will minister to you. For there are five trees for you in Paradise which remain undisturbed summer and winter and whose leaves do not fall. Whoever becomes acquainted with them will not experience death."*

not experience death: 1, 19, 85. origin motif: 18, 49, 50, 84. stones: 13.

(20) The disciples said to Jesus, "Tell us what the kingdom of heaven is like."

not experience death: 1, 18, 85. 20 once with 8 and 9. Motif link: trees (19) and field (21)?

He said to them, "It is like a mustard seed. It is the smallest of all seeds. But when it falls on tilled soil, it produces a great plant and becomes a shelter for birds of the sky."

(21)(a) Mary said to Jesus, "Whom are your disciples like?"

He said, "They are like children who have settled in a field which is not theirs. When the owners of the field come, they will say, 'Let us have back our field.' They (will) undress in their presence in order to let them have back their field and to give it back to them.

(b) "Therefore, I say, if the owner of a house knows that the thief is coming, he will begin his vigil before he comes and will not let him dig through into his house of his domain to carry away his goods. You, then, be on your guard against the world. Arm yourselves with great strength lest the robbers find a way to come to you, for the difficulty which you expect will (surely) materialize.

21b once separate, moved here; catch-word "owner."

(c) "Let there be among you a man of understanding. When the grain ripened, he came quickly with his sickle in hand and reaped it. Whoever has ears to hear, let him hear."

(22)(a) Jesus saw infants being suckled. He said to his disciples, "These infants being suckled are like those who enter the kingdom."

catchword "king-dom"; children motif link with 22a.

(b) They said to him, "Shall we *then, as children,* enter the kingdom?"

Jesus said to them, "When you make the two one, *and when you make the inside like the outside and the outside like the inside, and the above like the below, and when you make the male and the female one and the same,* so that the male not be male nor the female female; *and when you fashion eyes in place of an eye, and a hand in place of a hand, and a foot in place of a foot, and a likeness in place of a likeness;* then you will enter [the kingdom]."

one and the same, single one: 4, 23, 30 (POxy 1).

likeness: image 50, 83, 84.

22b. From *The Gospel of the Egyptians:* "When Salome asked when what she had inquired about would be known, the Lord said, 'When you have trampled on the garment of shame and when the two become one and the female (is) neither male nor female' " (source: Clement of Alexandria).

22b. From 2 *Clement*, a mid-second-century sermon: "For the Lord himself, on being asked by someone when his kingdom should come, said: 'When the two shall become one and that which is without as that which is within, and the male with the female neither male nor female.' "

(23) Jesus said, "I shall choose you, one out of thousand, and two out of ten thousand, *and they shall stand as a single one.*"

(24) *His disciples said to him, "Show us the place where you are, since it is necessary for us to seek it."*

He said to them, "Whoever has ears, let him hear. There is light within a man of light, and he lights up the whole world. If he does not shine, he is darkness."

(25) Jesus said, "Love your brother like your soul, guard him like the pupil of your eye."

(26) Jesus said, "You see the mote in your brother's eye, but you do not see the beam in your own eye. When you cast the beam out of your own eye, then you will see clearly to cast the mote from your brother's eye."

(27) ⟨Jesus said,⟩ "If you do not fast as regards the world, you will not find the kingdom. If you do not observe the Sabbath as a Sabbath, you will not see the father."

(28) Jesus said, "I took my place in the midst of the world, and I appeared to them in flesh. I found all of them intoxicated; I found none of them thirsty. And my soul became afflicted for the sons of men, because they are blind in their hearts and do not have sight; for empty they came into the world, and empty too they seek to leave the world. But for the moment they are intoxicated. When they shake off their wine, then they will repent."

(29) *Jesus said, "If the flesh came into being because of spirit, it is a wonder. But if spirit came into being because of the body, it is a wonder of wonders. Indeed, I am amazed at how this great wealth has made its home in this poverty."*

(30) *Jesus said, "Where there are three gods, they are gods. Where there are two or one, I am with him."*

(31) Jesus said, "No prophet is accepted in

one and the same, single one: 4, 22b, 30 (POxy 1).
place(s): 4, 60, 64, 68.

Once apart, 25 and 26 joined by "brother," "eye" catchwords.

Once apart, 27 and 28 joined by catchword "world."
literally, "I took my stand."

catchword "flesh."
body/flesh: 87, 112.

wealth: 85
poverty: 3b
[Coptic garbled; see POxy 1 30.]

Sayings 31–42 were

(30) POxy 1: (a) "[Jesus said], 'Where there are [three], they are without God, and where there is but [a single one], I say that I am with [him]. (b) Lift up the stone, and you will find me there. Split the piece of wood, and I am there'" (see 77b).

his own village; no physician heals those who know him."

(32) Jesus said, "A city being built on a high mountain and fortified cannot fall, nor can it be hidden."

(33) Jesus said, "Preach from your housetops that which you will hear in your ear. For no one lights a lamp and puts it under a bushel, nor does he put it in a hidden place, but rather he sets it on a lampstand so that everyone who enters and leaves will see its light."

(34) Jesus said, "If a blind man leads a blind man, they will both fall into a pit."

(35) Jesus said, "It is not possible for anyone to enter the house of a strong man and take it by force unless he binds his hands; then he will (be able to) ransack his house."

(36) Jesus said, "Do not be concerned from morning until evening and from evening until morning about what you will wear."

(37) His disciples said, "When will you become revealed to us and when shall we see you?"

Jesus said, "When you disrobe without being ashamed and take up your garments and place them under your feet like little children and tread on them, then [will you see] the son of the living one, and you will not be afraid."

(38) Jesus said, "Many times have you desired to hear these words which I am saying to you, and you have no one else to hear them from. There will be days when you will look for me and will not find me."

(39) Jesus said, "The pharisees and the

left in original order with no additions.

---

(31) POxy 1: "Jesus said, 'No prophet is accepted in his own country; no physician heals those who know him.' "

(36) POxy 1: "[Jesus said, 'Do not be concerned] from morning [until evening and] from evening [until] morning, neither [about] your [food] and what [you will] eat, [nor] about [your clothing] and what you [will] wear. [You are far] better than the [lilies] which [neither] card nor [spin]. As for you, when you have no garment, what [will you put on]? Who might add to your stature? He it is who who will give you your cloak.' "

scribes have taken the keys of knowledge and hidden them. They themselves have not entered, nor have they allowed to enter those who wish to. You, however, be as wise as serpents and as innocent as doves."

(40) Jesus said, "A grapevine has been planted outside of the father, but being unsound, it will be pulled up by its roots and destroyed."

(41) Jesus said, "Whoever has something in his hand will receive more, and whoever has nothing will be deprived of even the little he has."

(42) Jesus said, "Become passers-by."

(43) His disciples said to him, "Who are you, that you should say these things to us?"

〈Jesus said to them,〉 "You do not realize who I am from what I say to you, but you have become like the Jews, for they (either) love the tree and hate its fruit (or) love the fruit and hate the tree."

who are you?: 61b.

the Jews: John 5:16, 18, passim.

(44) Jesus said, "Whoever blasphemes against the father will be forgiven, and whoever blasphemes against the son will be forgiven, but whoever blasphemes against the holy spirit will not be forgiven either on earth or in heaven."

(45) Jesus said, "Grapes are not harvested from thorns, nor are figs gathered from thistles, for they do not produce fruit. A good man brings forth good from his storehouse; an evil man brings forth evil things from his evil storehouse, which is in his heart, and says evil things. For out of the abundance of the heart he brings forth evil things."

Moved here to have "says evil things" follow "blasphemy" saying.

(46) Jesus said, "Among those born of women, from Adam until John the Baptist, there is no one so superior to John the Baptist that his eyes should not be lowered (before him). Yet I have said, whichever one of you comes to be a child will be acquainted with the kingdom and will become superior to John."

(47) Jesus said, "It is impossible for a man to mount two horses or to stretch two bows. And it is impossible for a servant to serve two masters; otherwise, he will honor the one and treat the other contemptuously. No man drinks old wine and immediately desires to drink new wine. And new wine is not put into old wineskins, lest they burst; nor is old wine put into new wineskins, lest it spoil it. An old patch is not sewn onto a new garment, because a tear would result."

47 moved here. "Two horses," "two bows," and "two masters" act as catchwords with "two make peace" in 48.

(48) Jesus said, "If two make peace with each other in this one house, they will say to the mountain, 'Move away,' and it will move away."

(49) *Jesus said, "Blessed are the solitary and the elect, for you will find the kingdom. For you are from it, and to it you will return."*

solitary: 16, 75. origin motif: 18, 19, 50, 84.

(50) *Jesus said, "If they say to you, 'Where did you come from?', say to them, 'We came from the light, the place where the light came into being on its own accord and established [itself] and became manifest through their image. If they say to you, 'Is it you?', say, 'We are its children, and we are the elect of the living father.' If they ask you, 'What is the sign of your father in you?', say to them, 'It is a movement and repose.' "*

likeness, image: 22b, 83, 84.

living father: 3b. catchword "repose."

(51) His disciples said to him, "When will the repose of the dead come about, and when will the new world come?"

He said to them, "What you look forward to has already come, but you do not recognize it."

(52) His disciples said to him, "Twenty-four prophets spoke in Israel, and all of them spoke in you."

He said to them, "You have omitted the one living in your presence and have spoken (only) of the dead."

(53) His disciples said to him, "Is circumcision beneficial or not?"

He said to them, "If it were beneficial, their father would beget them already circumcised from their mother. Rather, the true circumcision in spirit has become completely profitable."

(54) Jesus said, "Blessed are the poor, for yours is the kingdom of heaven."

(55) Jesus said, "Whoever does not hate his father and mother cannot be a disciple to me. And whoever does not hate his brothers and sisters and take up his cross in my way will not be worthy of me."

(56) *Jesus said, "Whoever has come to understand the world has found (only) a corpse, and whoever has found a corpse is superior to the world."*

catchword "whoever.'
corpse: 60; see 80.

(57) Jesus said, "The kingdom of the father is like a man who had [good] seed. The man did not allow them to pull up the weeds; he said to them, 'I am afraid that you will go intending to pull up the weeds and pull up the wheat along with them. For on the day of the harvest the weeds will be plainly visible, and they will be pulled up and burned."

superior to world:
80, 111b.
57 once grouped
with 107 and 109.
"Man" is catchword
with 58.

(58) *Jesus said, "Blessed is the man who has suffered and found life."*

(59) *Jesus said, "Take heed of the living one while you are alive, lest you die and seek to see him and are unable to do so."*

catchwords "life" and
"living one"/"alive".

(60) ⟨They saw⟩ *a Samaritan carrying a lamb on the way to Judea. He said to his disciples, "That man is round about the lamb." They said to him, "So that he may kill it and eat it."*

60 is inserted between two sayings on dying.

He said to them, "While it is alive, he will not eat it, but only when he has killed it and it has become a corpse."

eat dead: 7, 11b.
corpse: 56.

They said to him, "He cannot do so otherwise."

He said to them, "You too, look for a place for yourselves within repose, lest you become a corpse and be eaten.

place(s): 4, 24, 64,
68.

(61)(a) Jesus said, "Two will rest on a bed; the one will die, and the other will live."

(b) Salome said, "Who are you, man, that you have come up on my couch and eaten from my table?"

Jesus said to her, "I am he who exists from

Rare catchword link
("bed"/"couch") by
second editor.

<u>the undivided. I was given some of the things
of my father."</u>

⟨...⟩ "I am your disciple." ⟨...⟩ <u>"Therefore, I
say, if he is destroyed, he will be filled with
light, but if he is divided, he will be filled with
darkness."</u>

(62) Jesus said, "It is to those [who are worthy of my] mysteries that I tell my mysteries.
Do not let your left hand know what your right
hand is doing."

(63) Jesus said, "There was a rich man who
had much money. He said, 'I shall put my
money to use so that I may sow, reap, plant,
and fill my storehouse with produce, with the
result that I shall lack nothing. Such were his
intentions, but that same night he died. Let
him who has ears hear."

(64) Jesus said, "A man had received visitors.
And when he had prepared the dinner, he sent
his servant to invite the guests. He went to the
first one and said to him, 'My master invites
you.' He said, 'I have claims against some merchants. They are coming to me this evening. I
must go and give them my orders. I ask to be
excused from the dinner.' He went to another
and said to him, 'My master has invited you.'
He said to him, 'I have just bought a house and
am required for the day. I shall not have any
spare time.' He went to another and said to
him. 'My master invites you.' He said to him,
'My friend is going to get married, and I am
to prepare the banquet. I shall not be able to
come. I ask to be excused from the dinner.' He
went to another and said to him. 'My master
invites you.' He said to him, 'I have just bought
a farm, and I am on my way to collect the rent.
I shall not be able to come. I ask to be excused.'
The servant returned and said to his master,
'Those whom you invited to the dinner have
asked to be excused.' The master said to his
servant, 'Go outside to the streets and bring
back those whom you happen to meet, so that

who are you?: 43.
things of father:
John 3:35; 6:15;
(6:37, 39).

they may dine.' *Businessmen and merchants [will] not enter the places of my father."*

(65) He said, "There was a good man who owned a vineyard. He leased it to tenant farmers so that they might work it and he might collect the produce from them. He sent his servants so that the tenants might give him the produce of the vineyard. They seized his servant and beat him, all but killing him. The servant went back and told his master. The master said, 'Perhaps he did not recognize them. He sent another servant. The tenants beat this one as well. Then the owner sent his son and said, 'Perhaps they will show respect to my son.' Because the tenants knew that it was he who was the heir to the vineyard, they seized him and killed him. Let him who has ears hear."

(66) Jesus said, "Show me the stone which the builders have rejected. That one is the cornerstone."

(67) Jesus said, "If one who knows the all still feels a personal deficiency, he is completely deficient."

(68) Jesus said, "Blessed are you when you are hated and persecuted. *Wherever you have been persecuted they will find no place."*

(69)(a) *Jesus said, "Blessed are they who have been persecuted within themselves. It is they who have truly come to know the father.*

(b) Blessed are the hungry, for the belly of him who desires will be filled."

(70) Jesus said, "That which you have will save you if you bring it forth from yourselves. That which you do not have within you [will] kill you if you do not have it within you."

(71) Jesus said, "I shall [destroy this] house, and no one will be able to build it [. . .]"

(72) [A man said] to him, "Tell my brothers to divide my father's possessions with me."

He said to him, "O man, who has made me a divider?"

place(s): 4, 24, 60, 68.

66 moved here by editor under influence of Mark 12:1–11?
the all: 2, 77.

place(s): 4, 24, 60, 64.
catchwords "blessed," "persecuted."

He turned to his disciples and said to them, "I am not a divider, am I?"

(73) Jesus said, "The harvest is great but the laborers are few. Beseech the lord, therefore, to send out laborers to the harvest."

(74) *He said, "O lord, there are many around the drinking trough, but there is nothing in the cistern."*

catchwords "lord" (73) and "many" (75)

(75) Jesus said, "Many are standing at the door, but it is *the solitary* who will enter the bridal chamber."

solitary: 16, 49.

(76) Jesus said, "The kingdom of father is like a merchant who had a consignment of merchandise and who discovered a pearl. That merchant was shrewd. He sold the merchandise and bought the pearl alone for himself. You too, seek his unfailing and enduring treasure where no moth comes near to devour and no worm destroys."

(77)(a) Jesus said, "It is I who am the light which is above them all. It is I who am the all. From me did the all come forth, and unto me did the all extend.

the all: 2, 67.
I am light: John 8:12; 9:5; 12:46.
77b—see POxy 1 (30).

(b) Split a piece of wood, and I am there. Lift up the stone, and you will find me there.

(78) Jesus said, "Why have you come out into the desert? To see a reed shaken by the wind? And to see a man clothed in fine garments [like your] kings and your great men? Upon them are fine garments, and they are unable to discern the truth."

(79) A woman from the crowd said to him, "Blessed are the womb which bore you and the breasts which nourished you."

He said to [her], "Blessed are those who have heard the word of the father and have truly kept it. For there will be days when you will say, 'Blessed are the womb which has not conceived and the breasts which have not given milk.' "

catch motif "body."; links 80 to 79.
superior to world: 56, 111b.

(80) *Jesus said, "He who has recognized the world has found the body, but he who has found the body is superior to the world."*

(81) Jesus said, "Let him who has grown rich

be king, and let him who possesses power renounce it."

(82) Jesus said, "He who is near me is near
the fire, and he who is far from me is far from
the kingdom."

(83) *Jesus said, "The images are manifest to man,
but the light in them remains concealed in the image
of the light of the father. He will become manifest,
but his image will remain concealed by his light."*

likeness, image: 22b,
50, 84.

(84) *Jesus said, "When you see your likeness, you
rejoice. But when you see your images which came
into being before you, and which neither die nor become manifest, how much will you have to bear?"*

likeness, image: 22b,
50, 83. origin motif:
18, 19, 49, 50.

(85) *Jesus said, "Adam came into being from a
great power and a great wealth, but he did not become worthy of you. For had he been worthy, [he
would] not [have experienced] death."*

wealth: 29.
not experience
death: 1, 18, 19.

(86) Jesus said, "[The foxes have their holes]
and the birds have their nests, but the son of
man has no place to lay his head and rest."

(87) *Jesus said, "Wretched is the body that is dependent upon a body, and wretched is the soul that
is dependent on these two."*

body/flesh: 29, 112.
soul: 112. catch mo-
tif "two" with angels
and prophets ?

(88) Jesus said, "The angels and the prophets will come to you and give you those things
you (already) have. And you too, give them
those things which you have, and say to yourselves, 'When will they come and take what is
theirs?' "

(89) Jesus said, "Why do you wash the outside of the cup? Do you not realize that he who
made the inside is the same one who made the
outside?"

(90) Jesus said, "Come unto me, for my yoke
is easy and my lordship is mild, and you will
find repose for yourselves."

(91) They said to him, "Tell us who you are
so that we may believe in you."

He said to them, "You read the face of the
sky and of the earth, but you have not recognized the one who is before you, and you do
not know how to read this moment."

(92) Jesus said, "Seek and you will find. Yet,

what you asked me about in former times and which I did not tell you then, now I do desire to tell, but you do not inquire after it."

(93) ⟨Jesus said,⟩ "Do not give what is holy to dogs, lest they throw them on the dung heap. Do not throw the pearls [to] swine, lest they . . . it [. . .]."

(94) Jesus [said], "He who seeks will find, and [he who knocks] will be let in."

(95) *[Jesus said], "If you have money, do not lend it at interest, but give [it] to one from whom you will not get it back."*

no catchword, but a pairing interrupted here.

(96) Jesus said, "The kingdom of the father is like [a certain] woman. She took a little leaven, [concealed] it in some dough, and made it into large loaves. Let him who has ears hear."

(97) Jesus said, "The kingdom of the [father] is like a certain woman who was carrying a [jar] full of meal. While she was walking [on the] road, still some distance from home, the handle of the jar broke and the meal emptied out behind her [on] the road. She did not realize it; she had noticed no accident. When she reached her house, she set the jar down and found it empty."

(98) Jesus said, "The kingdom of the father is like a certain man who wanted to kill a powerful man. In his house he drew his sword and stuck it into the wall in order to find out whether his hand could carry through. Then he slew the powerful man."

(99) The disciples said to him, "Your brothers and your mother are standing outside."

He said to them, "Those here who do the will of my father are my brothers and my mother. It is they who will enter the kingdom of my father."

(100) *They showed Jesus a gold coin and said to him, "Caesar's men demand taxes from us."*

He said to them, "Give Caesar what belongs to Caesar, give God what belongs to God, and give me what is mine."

no catchword, unless "mine-me" (with 101).

(101) ⟨Jesus said,⟩ "Whoever does not hate his [father] and his mother as I do cannot become a [disciple] to me. And whoever does [not] love his [father and] his mother as I do cannot become a [disciple to] me. For my mother [. . .], but [my] true [mother] gave me life."

(102) Jesus said, "Woe to the pharisees, for they are like a dog sleeping in the manger of oxen, for neither does he eat nor does he [let] the oxen eat."

(103) Jesus said, "Fortunate is the man who knows where the brigands will enter, so that [he] may get up, muster his domain, and arm himself before they invade."

or, "Blessed is . . . "

(104) They said to Jesus, "Come, let us pray today and let us fast."

Jesus said, "What is the sin that I have committed, or wherein have I been defeated? But when the bridegroom leaves the bridal chamber, then let them fast and pray."

(105) Jesus said, "He who knows the father and the mother will be called the son of a harlot."

(106) Jesus said, "When you make the two one, you will become the sons of man, and when you say, 'Mountain, move away,' it will move away."

(107) Jesus said, "The kingdom is like a shepherd who had a hundred sheep. One of them, the largest, went astray. He left the ninety-nine and looked for that one until he found it. When he had gone to such trouble, he said to the sheep, 'I care for you more than the ninety-nine.' "

(108) Jesus said, "He who will drink from my mouth will become like me. I myself shall become he, and the things that are hidden will be revealed to him."

108 once preceded 107 but was moved here for catchword link to "hidden" in 109. 57 probably once was in this parable group.

(109) Jesus said, "The kingdom is like a man who had a [hidden] treasure in his field without knowing it. And [after] he died, he left it to his [son]. The son [did] not know (about the

treasure). He inherited the field and sold [it]. And the one who bought it went plowing and [found] the treasure. He began to lend money at interest to whomever he wished."

(110) Jesus said, "Whoever finds the world and becomes rich, let him renounce the world."

(111)(a) Jesus said, "The heavens and the earth will be rolled up in your presence. And the one who lives from the living one will not see death."

(b) *Does not Jesus say, "Whoever finds himself is superior to the world?"*

(112) *Jesus said, "Woe to the flesh that depends on the soul; woe to the soul that depends on the flesh."*

(113) His disciples said to him, "When will the kingdom come?"

⟨Jesus said,⟩ "It will not come by waiting for it. It will not be a matter of saying 'here it is' or 'there it is.' Rather, the kingdom of the father is spread out upon the earth, and men do not see it."

(114) *Simon Peter said to them, "Let Mary leave us, for women are not worthy of life."*

Jesus said, "I myself shall lead her in order to make her male, so that she too may become a living spirit resembling you males. For every woman who will make herself male will enter the kingdom of heaven."

*The Gospel
According to Thomas*

Bibliography

BASIC REFERENCE

Biblical Archeologist, Fall 1979. The issue is devoted entirely to the Nag Hammadi discovery, including two fact-filled articles by Robinson.

Cameron, Ron, ed. *The Other Gospels; Non-Canonical Gospel Texts*. Philadelphia: Westminster, 1982.

Doresse, Jean. *The Secret Books of the Egyptian Gnostics: An Introduction to the Gnostic Coptic Manuscripts Discovered at Chenoboskion*. New York: Viking, 1960. Doresse's story of the discovery and his translation of *The Gospel of Thomas*.

Foerster, Werner, ed. *Gnosis, a Selection of Gnostic Texts, Patristic Evidence*, Vol. 1. Oxford: Clarendon Press, 1972.

Funk, Robert W., ed. *New Gospel Parallels*. Vols. 1 and 2. Philadelphia: Fortress, 1985. Parallel sayings not only among the New Testament Gospels but also with noteworthy apocryphal works, including *The Gospel of Thomas*, *The Dialogue of the Savior* and *The Apocryphon of James*.

Hedrick, Charles W., and Robert Hodgson, Jr., eds. *Nag Hammadi, Gnosticism, and Early Christianity*. Peabody, MA: Hendrickson, 1986. Fourteen scholars' papers at a 1983 conference.

Layton, Bentley. *The Gnostic Scriptures*. Garden City, NY: Doubleday, 1987. Includes new translations of many Nag Hammadi texts and church father reports.

————, ed. *The Rediscovery of Gnosticism; Proceedings of the International Conference on Gnosticism at Yale, New Haven, Connecticut. March 28–31, 1978*. 2 vols. Leiden: E. J. Brill, 1980–81.

Pagels, Elaine. *The Gnostic Gospels*. New York: Random House, 1979.

Perkins, Pheme. *The Gnostic Dialogue: The Early Church and the Crisis of Gnosticism*. New York: Paulist Press, 1980.

Robinson, James M., ed. *The Nag Hammadi Library in English*. Third rev. ed., San Francisco: Harper & Row, 1988. More than any other book, this could serve as a companion volume to my effort. Robinson provides a general introduction, managing editor Richard Smith writes about latter-day interpretations of Gnosticism, and a range of scholars give short introductions to each work from Nag Hammadi and two treatises at the Berlin Museum not duplicated in the Nag Hammadi collection.

Robinson, James M., and Helmut Koester. *Trajectories Through Early Christianity*. Philadelphia: Fortress, 1971.

Rudolph, Kurt. *Gnosis: The Nature and History of Gnosticism*. San Francisco: Harper & Row, 1977.

Scholer, David. *Nag Hammadi Bibliography, 1948–1969*. Leiden: E. J. Brill, 1971. Supplemented annually in the journal *Novum Testamentum*.

OTHER WORKS CONSULTED

Attridge, Harold W. "The Gospel of Thomas." In *Harper's Bible Dictionary*, edited by Paul J. Achtemeier. San Francisco: Harper & Row, 1985.

———. "The *Gospel of Truth* as an Exoteric Text." In *Nag Hammadi, Gnosticism and Early Christianity*, edited by Charles W. Hedrick and Robert Hodgson, Jr. Peabody, MA: Hendrickson, 1986.

———. "The Original Text of *Gos. Thom.*, Saying 30." *Bulletin of the American Society of Papyrologists* 16 (1979): 3.

Bianchi, Ugo, ed. *Le Origini Dello Gnosticismo: Colloquio di Messina, 13–18 Aprile 1966*. Leiden: E. J. Brill, 1970.

Bohle, Bruce, ed. *The Home Book of American Quotations*. New York: Dodd, Mead & Co., 1967.

Buckley, Jorunn Jacobson. "A Cult-Mystery in The *Gospel of Philip*." In *Journal of Biblical Literature* (December 1980).

Bultmann, Rudolf. *Primitive Christianity in Its Contemporary Setting*. Translated by R. H. Fuller. Cleveland: World Publishing, Living Age/Meridian paperback, 1956.

Cameron, Ron. *Sayings Traditions in the Apocryphon of James, Harvard Theological Studies 34*. Philadelphia: Fortress, 1984.

Ceram, C. W. *Gods, Graves, and Scholars*. Rev. ed. New York: Alfred A. Knopf, [1951] 1967.

Cohen, Martin A. "As Jewish History." In *The Bible in Modern Scholarship*, edited by J. Philip Hyatt. Nashville and New York: Abingdon, 1965.

Cross, Frank L., ed. *The Jung Codex, a newly recovered Gnostic papyrus; three studies*. London, Mowbray, New York: Morehouse-Gorham, 1955.

Crossan, John Dominic. *Four Other Gospels, Shadows on the Contours of Canon*. Minneapolis: Winston Press, 1985.

Davies, Stevan L. *The Gospel of Thomas and Christian Wisdom*. New York: Seabury Press, 1983.

Doresse, Jean. "A Gnostic Library from Upper Egypt." *Archeology* (Summer 1950).

Fitzmyer, Joseph A. "The Gnostic Gospels According to Pagels." *America* (Feb. 16, 1983).

_____. *Essays on the Semitic Background of the New Testament.* Chico, CA: Scholar's Press, 1974.

Gaertner, Bertil. *The Theology of the Gospel According to Thomas.* New York: Harper & Row, 1961.

Grant, Robert M. "Gnosticism." In *The New Encyclopedia Britannica Macropaedia.* Chicago: Encyclopedia Britannica, 1974.

_____. *Gnosticism and Early Christianity.* New York and London: Columbia University Press, 1959, 1966.

_____. "Gnostic Origins and the Basilideans of Irenaeus." *Virgiliae Christianae* 13 (1959).

Graves, Robert, and Raphael Patati. *Hebrew Myths: The Book of Genesis.* New York: McGraw-Hill, 1966.

Guillaumont, A., H.-Ch. Puech, G. Quispel, W. Till, and Yassah 'Abd Al Masih. *The Gospel According to Thomas.* Leiden: E. J. Brill; New York: Harper & Row, 1959.

Hedrick, Charles W. "Kingdom Sayings and Parables of Jesus in the *Apocryphon of James*: Tradition and Redaction." *New Testament Studies* 29 (1983).

Helmbold, A. K. *The Nag Hammadi Gnostic Texts and the Bible.* Grand Rapids: Baker, 1967.

Hennecke, Edgar; edited by Wilhelm Schnéemelcher. *New Testament Apocrypha: Vol. 1: Gospels and Related Writings.* Philadelphia: Westminster, 1963.

Herford, R. Travers. *Pirke Aboth, The Ethics of the Talmud: Sayings of the Fathers. Text, Complete Translation and Commentaries.* New York: Schocken Books, 1962.

Jonas, Hans. "Response to G. Quispel's 'Gnosticism and the New Testament.' " In *The Bible in Modern Scholarship,* edited by J. Philip Hyatt. Nashville and New York: Morehouse-Gorham, 1955.

_____. *The Gnostic Religion: The Message of the Alien God and the Beginnings of Christianity.* Boston: Beacon Press, 1958, 1963.

Jung, Carl G. *Memories, Dreams, Reflections,* recorded and edited by Aniela Jaffe. New York: Pantheon, 1961.

_____. *The Collected Works of C. G. Jung.* Translated by R. F. C. Hull, vol. 9, part II. New York: Pantheon, 1959.

Koester, Helmut. "Apocryphal and Canonical Gospels." *Harvard Theological Review* (January–April 1980).

_____. "Gnostic Sayings and Controversy Traditions in John 8:12–59." In *Nag Hammadi, Gnosticism and Early Christianity,* edited by Charles W. Hedrick and Robert Hodgson, Jr. Peabody, MA: Hendrickson, 1986.

_____. *Introduction to the New Testament,* vol. 2, *History and Literature of Early Christianity.* Philadelphia: Fortress, 1982.

MacRae, George. "The Coptic Gnostic *Apocalypse of Adam.*" *The Heythrop Journal* 6 (1965).

———. "Biblical News: Gnosis in Messina." *Catholic Biblical Quarterly* XXVIII (1966).

———. "The *Apocalypse of Adam* Reconsidered." In *Society of Biblical Literature Proceedings, vol. 2, Sept. 1–5, 1972, Los Angeles.* Missoula, MT: Scholars Press, 1972.

———. "Seth in Gnostic Texts and Traditions." *Society of Biblical Literature 1977 Seminar Papers,* edited by Paul J. Achtemeier. Missoula, MT: Scholars Press, 1977.

———. "Apocalypse of Adam." In *The Old Testament Pseudepigrapha, Apocalyptic Literature & Testaments,* edited by James H. Charlesworth. Garden City, NY: Doubleday, 1983.

Meeks, Wayne A. "The Image of the Androgyne: Some Uses of a Symbol in Earliest Christianity." *History of Religions* 13 (1974).

Menard, Jacques E. "Thomas, Gospel of." In *The Interpreter's Dictionary of the Bible, Supplementary Volume,* edited by Keith Crum. Nashville: Abingdon, 1976.

Meyer, Marvin W., trans. *The Secret Teachings of Jesus, Four Gnostic Gospels.* New York: Random House, 1984.

Neusner, Jacob. " 'Pharisaic-Rabbinic' Judaism: A Clarification." *History of Religions* (Feb. 1973).

Pagels, Elaine, with Helmut Koester. "Report on the *Dialogue of the Savior* (CG III,5)." In *Nag Hammadi and Gnosis, Papers read at the First International Congress of Coptology (Cairo, December 1976),* edited by R. McL. Wilson. Leiden: E. J. Brill, 1978.

———. *The Gnostic Jesus and Early Christian Politics.* Department of Religious Studies, Arizona State University. Tempe, AZ: Arizona State, 1981.

Pearson, Birger A. "Jewish Haggadic Traditions in the *Testimony of Truth* (CG IX,3)." In *Ex Orbe Religionum: Studia Geo Widengren.* Lugduni Batavorum: E. J. Brill, 1972.

———. "Friedlander Revisited: Alexandrian Judaism and Gnostic Origins." *Studia Philonica* II (1973).

———. "Nag Hammadi Codices." In *1974 Yearbook of the Encyclopedia Judaica.* Jerusalem: Keter Publishing House, 1974.

———. "Anti-Heretical Warnings in Codex IX from Nag Hammadi." In *Essays on the Nag Hammadi Text in Honor of Pahor Labib,* edited by Martin Krause. Leiden: E. J. Brill, 1975.

———. "Jewish Sources in Gnostic Literature." In *Society of Biblical Literature Seminar Papers Series,* edited by Kent Harold Richards. Atlanta, GA: Scholars Press, 1986. (Same article appears in *The Literature of the Jewish People in the Period of the Second Temple and the Talmud, vol. 2, Jewish Writings of the Second Temple Period,* edited by Michael Stone. Philadelphia: Fortress; Assen: Van Gorcum, 1984.)

Perkins, Pheme. "*Apocalypse of Adam*: The Genre and Function of a Gnostic Apocalypse." *Catholic Biblical Quarterly* 39 (1977).

_____. "Johanine Traditions in *Ap. Jas.* (NHC I,2)." *Journal of Biblical Literature* 101 (Sept. 1982).

Perrin, Norman. *Rediscovering the Teaching of Jesus.* New York: Harper & Row, 1967.

Quispel, Gilles. "Gnosticism and the New Testament." In *The Bible in Modern Scholarship,* edited by J. Philip Hyatt. Nashville and New York: Morehouse-Gorham, 1955.

_____. "Jung and the Jung Codex." Paper at the Panorion Conference, Los Angeles, Sept. 5, 1975.

Robinson, James M. *The Nag Hammadi Codices, a general introduction to the nature and significance of the Coptic Gnostic Library from Nag Hammadi.* 2nd rev. ed. Claremont: Institute for Antiquity and Christianity, 1977.

_____. "The Jung Codex: The Rise and Fall of a Monopoly." *Religious Studies Review* 3 (1977).

_____. *The Problem of History in Mark and Other Marcan Studies.* Philadelphia: Fortress, 1982.

Russell, David Syne. *The Method and Message of Jewish Apocalyptic 200 B.C.-A.D. 100. Philadelphia: Westminster, 1964.*

Schoedel, William R. "Naassene Themes in the Coptic *Gospel of Thomas.*" *Vigiliae Christianae* 14 (1960).

Scholem, Gershom. *Major Trends in Jewish Mysticism.* New York: Schocken Books, 1961.

Smith, Jonathan Z. "The Garments of Shame." *History of Religion* 5 (1965).

_____. "Hellenistic Religions." In *The New Encyclopedia Britannica, Macropaedia.* Chicago: Encyclopedia Britannica, 1974.

Turner, John D. "Sethian Gnosticism: A Literary History." In *Nag Hammadi, Gnosticism and Early Christianity,* edited by Charles W. Hedrick and Robert Hodgson, Jr. Peabody, MA: Hendrickson, 1986.

Vree, Dale. "Biblical Revisionism." *National Catholic Reporter* (Feb. 17, 1980).

Wilson, Robert. *Gnosis and the New Testament.* Philadelphia: Fortress, 1968.

Wintermute, Orval. "A Study of Gnostic Exegesis of the Old Testament." In *The Use of the Old Testament in the New and Other Essays: Studies in Honor of William Franklin Stinespring,* edited by J. M. Efird. Durham: Duke University Press, 1972.

Wisse, Frederick. "The Redeemer Figure in the Paraphrase of Shem." *Novum Testamentum* XII (1970).

_____. "The Nag Hammadi Library and the Heresiologists." *Vigiliae Christianae* 25 (1971).

Yadin, Yigael. *The Message of the Scrolls.* New York: Simon and Schuster, 1957.

Yamauchi, Edwin M. *Pre-Christian Gnosticism: A Survey of the Proposed Evidences*. Grand Rapids, MI: Eerdmans, 1973.

Zandee, Jan. "Gnostic Ideas on the Fall and Salvation." *Numen* 11 (1964).

Index

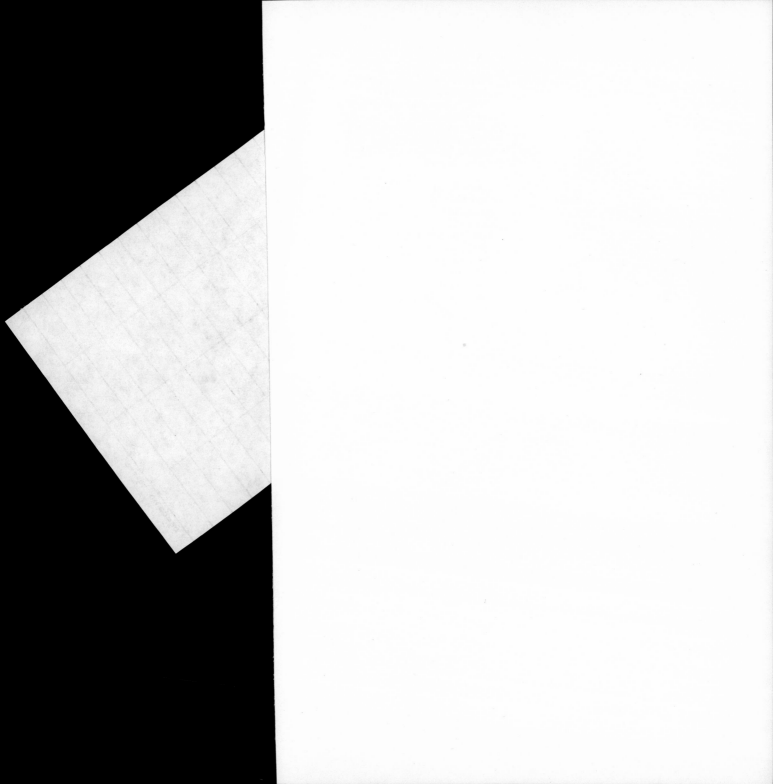

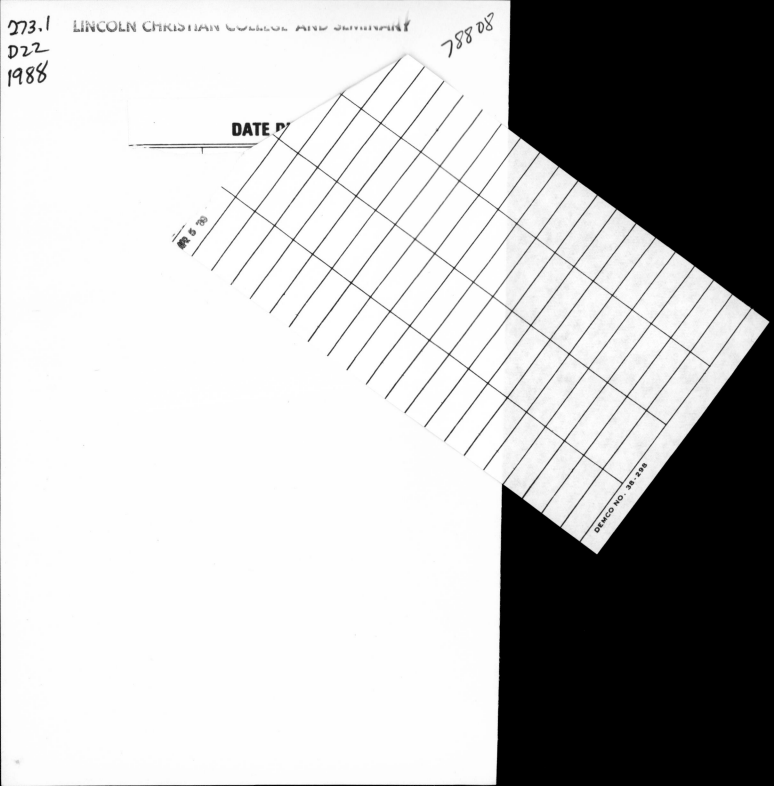